Lessons in Leadership

Lessons in Leadership

Updated and Expanded

William Fisher
Charles Bernstein

VNR VAN NOSTRAND REINHOLD
New York

Van Nostrand Reinhold
115 Fifth Avenue
New York, New York 10003

Chapman and Hall
2-6 Boundary Row
London, SE1 8HN, England

Thomas Nelson Australia
102 Dodds Street
South Melbourne 3205
Victoria, Australia

Nelson Canada
1120 Birchmount Road
Scarborough, Ontario MIK 5G4, Canada

16 15 14 13 12 11 10 9 8 7 6 5 4 3 2 1

Table of Contents

Preface

In this book we've asked a lot of questions of a lot of people, so let us open with a question to you. How do you define the hospitality industry? First, it's quite likely that you began to segment the components of the industry defining it in terms of its aggregate constituent parts, such as restaurants, hotels/motels, clubs, resorts, airlines, amusement parks, et al. You are quite correct in doing so, as these specific lines of business are customarily considered to be part of the hospitality industry. Perhaps you took it a step further and also considered the vertical business linkages as part of the industry such as distributors, food, equipment, and supplies manufacturers; and service providers such as consultants, trade press, associations, etc. You can make a persuasive argument that the hospitality industry is inclusive of these components as well. Finally, and depending on your experience and perspective, your definition could include not-for-profit organizations such as colleges and universities, hospitals, (after all, the word "hospital" is embraced by the larger word "hospitality") and so forth. We think you are quite right to integrate all of the foregoing into the concept of the hospitality industry for our own definition is at once simple but poignant. The hospitality industry is the care and feeding of people who are away from home, and its resources are those organizations with their millions of dedicated employees who play a role at one point or another in the process of providing facilities, food, and services to enhance the well-being of others.

By any measure, the hospitality industry has enjoyed tremendous success over the past three decades, and the good news is that future projections point to even greater growth as we head toward the 21st century. The reasons for this propitious forecast are well known (more working women, a more active, mobile population, a shifting from a production to a service economy, etc.) and have been well documented.

Our purpose is not to repeat them in this book, but rather our purpose is to tap the minds of some of the most successful hospitality industry leaders of the present day to gain insight into their core thinking, values, perspectives, management styles, personal and professional standards, and creative instincts that has resulted in their achieving significant leadership responsibilities for themselves, their businesses, and the industry to which they have chosen to devote their lives. These men and women who have participated with us in compiling this book are too valuable a resource to posterity not to have their thoughts recorded. They are uncommon people.

We contacted well over 100 industry leaders and asked each to respond to one question in an "up close and personal manner" anchoring their replies to the tenets of the concept of leadership. Thus, the title of this book, *Lessons In Leadership: Perspectives for Hospitality Industry Success*. We think you will enjoy and benefit from what they say, as we did.

Charles Bernstein   Bill Fisher

Expect Competition,
But Be Wary Of Imitators

Guss Dussin is President of OSF International, a chain of pasta restaurants doing business as The Old Spaghetti Factory, headquartered in Portland, Oregon. He is a director of the National Restaurant Association.

Question: If you could live your career over again, what would you do differently and why?

In addressing the question, the first thing that came to mind was that I would have started The Old Spaghetti Factory when I was 21 years old rather than 43. But that would mean that I would have missed out on the learning process I went through for 20 years working for my father and my two uncles. Most of their adult lives they were in the restaurant business and, at an early age, I was exposed to the business and started bussing tables when I was 14. So, I believe it's fair to say that The Old Spaghetti Factory is the direct result of all of the experiences and all of the lessons that my father and my uncles learned from 1914 to when they opened their first restaurant in Portland and passed it on to me. When I came along in 1947 and went to work for them, they had already been in business for 33 years.

I am sure that attending an H.R.I. program would have given me an overview of the industry and the business and, possibly, would have sped up the pace of my understanding and my grasp of what it takes to be in the restaurant business. However, I do not think that I would change the way I learned the basics of what it took to be successful in the restaurant business, because the Virginia Cafe survived for over 60 years in the same location which meant that there were some basic fundamentals there that had real staying power. The Old Spaghetti Factory idea, when it came up and was seriously considered as achievable, would always

3

cause me to refer back to my experience in running my father's restaurant and the other restaurants with which I had become involved. Those lessons, learned the hard way and certainly the long way, served me in good stead when it came time to sit down and make the hundreds and hundreds of decisions that have to be made when you decide to execute a new concept.

When you decide to open a restaurant, in whatever size, shape, or form, the most difficult thing is that you must go over, point by point, every item involved with the opening of that restaurant: where to locate, what to serve, what kind of price range, etc. It goes on and on. For instance, what type of waiter/waitress are you going to hire? Are you going to have a person that is dressed in a tuxedo, are you going to hire an experienced waitress who has worked in a restaurant for 20 or 30 years and is a professional, or are you going to take the approach of hiring untrained young people and turning them into skilled waiters and waitresses who really care about the customer.

One thing for certain that I would not change is the two or three years preceding the opening of The Old Spaghetti Factory and the five to ten years after the opening of The Old Spaghetti Factory. It was sheer fun and excitement, and we had a feeling of doing something different and worthwhile. I cannot think of enough adjectives to describe the tremendous feeling of elation that existed in all who were involved when we discovered that we had somehow run into a wonderful idea, and that it worked, and that we could continue to grow and expand. Then came the realization that the techniques and the skills that I had acquired in the twenty years that I had worked for my father and for myself in running a coffee shop-type restaurant did not prepare me or qualify me for the challenges of running multiple units. That, again, is something that in hindsight you could say "if I had it to do over again," I would have taken courses in business law, accounting, finance, corporate structuring and management, and in communications, and marketing. In other words, that is where the formal education would have really come into play, but I had to learn it and do it through on-the-job training. Maybe, in a way, that was the best education. Also, the shifting of emphasis from being an entrepreneur and flying by the seat of my pants to becoming a manager was an interesting process requiring much adjustment and painful self-examination. This led to our hiring an outside corporate manager who helped redefine our culture, set up in-depth training programs, and transformed The Old Spaghetti Factory from a mostly one-man show into a solid team oriented company.

And, I have also found tremendous satisfaction in watching the growth of some of our top people who started with the Company as busboys or waiters and who now hold positions of responsibility at corporate headquarters.

Another area that I certainly could improve on the second time around would be in the way that I handled the real estate that came with our stores. We had the opportunity several times to make purchases and chose not to, primarily because we did not feel we had the resources to both expand our units and be able to acquire the real estate underneath those units. Being rather cautious in nature, it was always in the back of my mind that if you had a unit that did not perform, at least you could take your lumps with that particular store and walk away from it. But, if you owned the real estate you had to take double lumps because you would not only have a sick store on your hands, you would also have a sick piece of real estate. That was one of the major reasons we chose not to purchase the real estate in the early years. In hindsight, of course, I would say that was a mistake and we could certainly have made some very good acquisitions since we were pioneers in many of the locations that we leased.

The other obvious regret is that I did not have the vision to expand faster. It would certainly be a priority if you would say to me, "live your career over again," to reach out to as many major markets as quickly as possible in order to shut off the imitators and the copy cats. Competition is expected, but it is the imitators that you dread and try to short circuit by getting there first. I know, from talking to many people in the industry, that this is one thing that anyone who starts with an idea that is new, exciting and different is always concerned about: how quickly they can get up and running before the "me-too's" starting chewing away at them.

Some final thoughts — we are all given a finite time on this earth and we need to think about and grasp those opportunities when they show themselves. You need to trust your instincts and not be afraid to fail, and, of course, you must have the energy to carry out your plans. Many good ideas die young and any new project or idea takes a tremendous amount of energy, and you really must extend yourself if you are ever going to make it happen. It will not happen just by talking or indulging in wishful thinking or bouncing ideas off of your friends. If you are really serious and you feel that you have an idea and it is a great one, then you have got to set into motion the forces necessary, and you are the only one that can do that. The prime mover is responsible in brining about results. Sheer inertia shoots down most projects which start with, "Wouldn't it be great if . . ."

I wish that I had taken the plunge one or two more times. Maybe before my career comes to an end I can practice what I preach.

You Can Always Do It Better

Harris H. "Bud" Rusitzky is the President and Chief Executive Officer of Serv-Rite Foodservice and Consulting Corporation and Serv-Rite Vending Services located in Pittsford, New York, a suburb of Rochester. He served as the 1989-90 President of the National Restaurant Association.

Question: If you could live your career over again, what would you do differently, and why?

In answering this question my reflexive response is "I would do it exactly the same way." A little deeper thought, however, would make me think of all the things I wanted to do and the concepts that I had but didn't get done. If I could do it over again, I would put more emphasis in those areas. One concept we had was to take people from within the company and give them the skills to move into management positions. This worked extremely well for our company, but if I had to do it again I would spend more time, money, and energy in developing these people to an even higher skill level than we were able to take them. I would have provided better incentives for people to develop individually so that they could have not only the basic skills, but the skills that are really needed in our industry. Specifically, I would have had them better understand profit and loss statements and balance sheets, rather than just food cost, labor cost, and general expenses. We also should have had a psychologist or a behavioral science expert give seminars and offer consulting services. We needed an education program with our hospitality colleges. In the administrative area, at one time we had two Vice Presidents, one for operations and another for administrative development. When the Vice President for Administration left our company, I failed to replace him. In retrospect, it was not a good move.

7

There were all the reasons for not replacing him: no one met the standards, the search did not attract the right person, the timing was wrong, etc. We soon started to feel that we could get along without that position. That cost us, and myself, some missed opportunities.

A few years ago we starting a vending division because we were forced to do so. Once again, in hindsight, we should have started a vending division a long time ago. It would have made our company stronger and more diversified although the capital investment would have been much greater.

My early background with ARA had been strong in the health service segment of the industry. Because it was so time consuming and profits were minimal, I made the decision not to go into that arena when I started Serv-Rite. Once again, if I had to do it over again, I would have capitalized on my experiences and moved the company into the health segment of the industry.

Bonus and employee programs are always difficult. We tried to change our programs every three years to make them interesting and exciting. One year a bonus might be paid in silver dollars, one year in government bonds, one time we might have a party for our management team only. Later, we would have a family outing for all of our employees. This worked but, again, it would have worked better with some longer range planning and a more formalized approach.

In summary, the conclusion I draw is there were missed opportunities. Once your plans are set, it really pays to discipline yourself to look at them at least every six months and say, "Where are we going? Why aren't we going where we thought we were going? Why aren't we going at the pace that we thought we could go?" I am hoping that I will have the opportunity to teach in the hospitality industry some time in my life and be able to convey to the students of the hospitality industry the philosophy that could have made our company even greater than it is today. We have done it well, but we could have done it better.

Activate Your Dreams

Anthony Athanas is President of Anthony's Fine Restaurants, a Boston, Massachusetts, headquartered foodservice organization widely known for its award winning concepts. He is an honorary director of the National Restaurant Association.

Question: What is the most creative idea you have ever experienced in the hospitality industry?

Throughout the 1950's, my regular trips from my home in Swampscott on Boston's North Shore to St. George Cathedral, the Albanian Orthodox Church in South Boston, took me and my young family along the Boston waterfront which, at the time, was in a rather depressing state of disrepair.

Boston was just beginning to embark on the great resurgence which characterized its redevelopment in the late 1950's. The Prudential Center near the Back Bay of Boston — some distance from the historic waterfront — was on the drawing boards of the city planners and architects and was scheduled for completion in 1965.

The huge center would feature what was to be, for a lengthy period of time, the tallest (740 feet) building in Boston, the Prudential Tower, and a new Sheraton-Boston Hotel. In later years the Pru Tower would surrender its height advantage to the new John Hancock Tower a half a mile away.

Notwithstanding the tremendous development impetus these insurance companies gave the Back Bay-Copley Square area, I still clung to the feeling, to the hope that Boston's historic waterfront would eventually witness an even greater development.

The city of Boston, once the leading port on the East Coast, had long since surrendered this position to New York.

Now the many docks and piers along Atlantic and Northern avenues were rotting and, for the most part, in such a sad state that one had to do much with the imagination to visualize the potential for new growth throughout the area.

The two avenues which meet at right angles near the point where Boston's heavily congested Central Artery emerges from the South Station tunnel were relics of the horse and buggy days. Their cobblestone surfaces did little to inspire optimism about future growth in the area.

But as I passed through the area almost weekly in the mid-1960's, I became more convinced about what the future would hold, and I made up my mind to construct a large new seafood restaurant somewhere along the waterfront.

Boston had its share of seafood eating places, but I had in mind an establishment that would rank as the leading waterfront restaurant in the world.

I looked over several harbor pier properties along Atlantic Avenue before singling out the dilapidated Pier Four on Northern Avenue as the site for fulfillment of my lifelong dream.

The vista from the end of the pier spanned an arc which included Boston's downtown skyline and went all the way around to the magnificient view of Boston's Logan International Airport which was about to undergo an expansion that would make it one of the world's busiest airports.

Many of my friends and associates on the North Shore of Boston where I had three excellent restaurants thought my common sense had taken leave of me and advised me against getting "in over my head." Even my dear wife, Esther, who knows me and my predilection for good timing, was skeptical.

The major Boston banks were reluctant to back me up, my past success on the North Shore notwithstanding. Finally, only by putting everything I had on the line including my home and three restaurants was I able to move ahead with a new restaurant on Pier Four.

Architectural and engineering planning began late in 1961. Tons and tons of hard fill had to be trucked in for the foundation work and the two acres of parking needed to accommodate the large patronage I envisioned.

Throughout much of 1960 and 1961, I was at the site almost every day watching my dream take shape and coping with the usual problems encountered on construction projects. Not the least of these problems was my apprehension about how well the restaurant, built by a North Shore newcomer to the Boston business scene, would be received by the public. I prayed that the large restaurant I was building on the Boston waterfront — one which featured fresh seafood, first class service, and a beautiful surrounding panaroma — would be a hit.

Days and months elapsed and Anthony's Pier Four Restaurant approached the point where I had to focus on the actual opening. I must confess that I was very nervous. All the resources that I had, all my dreams for my wife and four boys were tied up in my gamble.

But I was so busy around the clock in the fall of 1963 that I began to live on the excitement of the opening. And I grew more confident as I put together a large staff of chefs, cooks, waiters, and others in whose hands my future would depend once the opening gong rang.

Pier Four opened in October with a healthy gathering of people, and we have never looked back in the quarter of a century which has elapsed. In a relatively short period of time after the second floor was finished and opened for business, we had the distinction of having the biggest gross of any restaurant under one roof.

I was fortunate indeed. One always needs plenty of luck when undertaking a large venture, especially one into a new area where some resentment on the part of competitors is certain to manifest itself.

The message I am trying to convey is the need to persevere in your beliefs, your endeavors. We all make mistakes and God knows I have made my share, many more than I want to relate here. But, if you have an idea, a plan, a dream — call it what you will — don't be afraid to push ahead.

And remember that the public always wants and demands the best from you, no matter what your field of endeavor. Top quality day in and day out should be your standard modus operandi. And if you rest on your laurels, trouble is ahead just around the corner. To maintain a proper perspective on what you are doing, let me share with you some previous and memorable words of wisdom uttered by my late mother years ago at a large Athanas family get together. Many of my kinfolk, taken with my success as a restaurateur, were openly heaping praise on me and boasting about what a success I was.

My dear, aging mother listened for a while and then cautioned everyone with a rejoinder I have never forgotten:

"Too soon to tell," she said in her native Albanian tongue.

"Too soon to tell," she repeated, pointing her index finger at me.

And with those few pearls of speech, I was down off my high horse and back to earth where everything was in proper focus.

I commend these perceptive words to all of you.

A New Concept Is Born

William F. Regas is a partner in Regas, The Restaurant, The Gathering Place located in Knoxville, Tennessee. In 1982, he and other partners developed a new concept called Grady's Goodtimes. He is a past president of the National Restaurant Association.

Question: What is the most creative idea you have ever experienced in the hospitality industry?

The founding and developing of Grady's Goodtimes, Good Food & Drink is my most creative idea by far. My partners, Gus Regas and Frank Regas, Mike Connor, Rick Federico, and my son, Grady Regas, were all very instrumental in founding this restaurant from scratch in 1982. We first wrote out the business plan for the restaurant. We determined what kind of restaurant we wanted, our desired target market, the type of people we wanted to serve our guests, the atmosphere we wanted to create, and the type of food and beverages we wanted to serve. To preserve our passion for high quality, the food would be prepared in house from scratch. We envisioned a restaurant that would be "better and different", in which our friendly people would consistently demonstrate their pride through superior attention to detail in all aspects of the business.

I will share with you why we started the new restaurant concept, how we developed it as a team, and some of the human interest stories and the fun and hard work that have positively evolved Grady's over the years.

My cousins, Gus and Frank Regas, and I had been operating Regas Restaurant, a single full service restaurant which was founded by our fathers in 1919. We were motivated to start a new restaurant concept for several reasons. My son, Grady, was scheduled to graduate from college in 1981. He told us that he realized it would be difficult for all of us to make a living in just one family owned restaurant. If we would be interested in developing a new restaurant together, he wanted to be a partner. This was a strong motivation for Gus, Frank, and me. We had a lot of confidence in Grady as he had always been a leader during school and within the community.

We also got inspiration from ideas shared with us by fellow members of the National Restaurant Association during my year as President of the Association from May 1980 to May 1981. One of the benefits of the duties of being President of the National Restaurant Association is that there are many opportunities to travel and evaluate the most successful restaurants. During conversations with some of America's leading restaurateurs, there were many discussions about the coming trends for the 1980's and 1990's. These discussions helped us to focus ideas for Grady's Goodtimes. Fellow restaurateurs across America are very friendly, and most are willing to share their experiences and knowledge with others.

For several decades, the Regas family owned one and one-half acres of land in a good location in Knoxville. It was underdeveloped as a miniature golf course. We could envision a quality, casual restaurant and possibly a few shops in connection with or near the restaurant. A new restaurant concept would also give us the opportunity to develop this land to its highest and best use.

Robert Weir, our CPA, did a proforma at my request for the proposed new restaurant. The name of the restaurant on the proforma was "Grady's Cafe and Bar." One weekend in the summer of 1981, Grady and I went to a car wash on a Saturday afternoon. I presented him with this proforma. He looked it over carefully. By the time the car was clean, we had determined that it had great potential. We shook hands and said, "Let's go for it!"

Having agreed to do the new restaurant, the wheels began to turn in regard to the many necessary decisions that would create reality out of an idea. We thought it was extremely important to get a very creative architect who could design Grady's Goodtimes to be positioned at the top of the casual dining market segment. We asked Earl Swensson & Associates from Nashville, Tennessee to be our architect. They had previously done creative work for Opryland in Nashville.

We asked Mike Connor to join our team as President of Grady's and part owner. Mike was impressed with the plans and the ideas to develop a special casual restaurant built upon our old tradition of quality, service, cleanliness, and honest value. Mike agreed to become President of Grady's and lead the team in further developing the menu, recipes, and quality people that have made Grady's successful. He invited Rick Federico to join our management team and to also be part owner. Rick like Frank Regas had considerable knowledge and expertise in food. Their expertise was a great complement to the wine and beverage knowledge that Gus Regas contributed to our effort.

We had a lot of fun even though it was intense planning and work. We stressed from the beginning that we wanted to have a good time. While creating the menu, our young team tested all the products at Test Quality Assurance Workshops (TQAW) in the "Test Kitchen" (Grady's kitchen at home). We tested the various recipes and invited twenty people representative of our target market to come and evaluate the food.

Kevin Thompson completed our management team upon his arrival just prior to the opening of our first Grady's Goodtimes in Knoxville, Tennessee on December 1, 1982. Additional Grady's opened in Charlotte, North Carolina; Atlanta, Georgia; Birmingham, Alabama; Chattanooga, Tennessee; and Memphis, Tennessee. Our seventh Grady's will also be located in Knoxville, Tennessee, and opened in October, 1989.

Reflectively, Grady's Goodtimes was the right blend of ideas at just the right time. It provided a career opportunity for Grady as it will eventually for thousands of other Americans. It was the right solution for more appropriately developing the family's real estate. It was a perfect stage to execute our creativity and to demonstrate our love for the industry that has become our way of life.

In September 1988 at a Multi-Unit Food Service Organization Meeting in Washington, D.C., Mike Connor and I had the opportunity to meet with Norman Brinker, Chairman of Chili's, Inc. and Lane Cardwell, Vice President of Strategic Development for Chili's. Mike and I noted to Norman and Lane that we would be in Dallas in October, 1988, to attend a Shopping Center Development meeting. We were seeking locations for Grady's Goodtimes in the Southeast. They invited us to come to the Chili's Corporate Office during our trip. Mike and I gladly accepted their invitation. We welcomed their input and ideas on how to most successfully further expand Grady's Goodtimes. We had been building two restaurants a year and were thinking about increasing our growth rate to perhaps three a year.

After our Dallas Shopping Development Meeting, we went to Chili's Corporate Office and had the opportunity to meet with Lane Cardwell and Ron McDougall, President of Chili's. We shared our philosophies of managing restaurants. We agreed on the importance of selecting bright, enthusiastic people for our restaurants who in turn would also be able to select successful people. We observed that our philosophies of quality food, service, cleanliness, and good value were similar to Chili's. They stress having fun in their business, whereas, we stress having good times with our people and guests.

The philosophies and styles of management were uncannily similar and compatible, yet distinctively individualistic. Norman Brinker later joined our meeting and asked us about our plans. He had been told about our upscale, casual concept.

Chili's had been looking into developing a similar concept themselves or acquiring another restaurant concept that would be an upscale casual type. After some discussion, Norman saw the compatibility of philosophies and management style. He said, "Why don't we grow this concept together?" Our response was, "If it's mutually beneficial, then let's explore it." Norman said he could see tremendous possibilities and emphasized the extreme importance of timing. He said that if we're going to do it, we should proceed with negotiations and see if a synergistic merger could be accomplished.

Norman, Ron, Lane, and Jim Parish, Chili's Chief Financial Officer, came to Knoxville and presented a plan that could accelerate our growth within the Chili's organization and help us to reach our goals faster. Grady's Board of Directors accepted their proposal. On February 28, 1989 we merged with Chili's. The beauty of our marriage is that as we grow, we are reaffirming that Chili's and Grady's are indeed *better together.*

We are now accelerating our growth and development of people to operate additional Grady's Goodtimes throughout the country. Grady's will soon be serving in Plantation, Florida; Dallas, Texas; Little Rock, Arkansas; and Ft. Worth, Texas. It has been fun to be a part of the creative ideas with bright people, and to see Grady's grow and develop into one of the most successful concepts in America today.

My father, Frank, and his brother, George, told me when I was a teenager working the counter at Regas Restaurant, "In America you can do anything you want to do . . . Be anything you want to be as long as you try." I feel fortunate to have the opportunity to be in America to carry on the heritage of hospitality that my father began and to experience the process of how ideas and dreams can become positive realities.

Nobody's Perfect

Ted J. Balestreri is the co-founder and co-owner of The Sardine Factory, an award winning restaurant located in Monterey, California. It is part of the Restaurants Central Organization. Ted Balestreri is past President of the National Restaurant Association.

Question: If you could live your career over again, what would you do differently and why?

Although I can't help but feel the results of my 30 years in the restaurant business have been very successful, there are certain areas that I look back on and think I could have handled differently.

At the outset, my partner, Bert Cutino, and I were able to make all the management decisions on our own. Because we had only The Sardine Factory at the time, we were able to put a lot of time and energy into each and every important decision.

But when we started to grow and opened new restaurants, we didn't delegate the authority to a mid-management level to make decisions. As we grew, we moved a little farther away from the customer on a day-to-day basis, and the decisions took longer and longer to implement. We should have realized this sooner.

As a company grows and you plan for that from the beginning, it is important to build a management team and to provide the team with the tools and authority to make decisions on different levels. It's vital to give a clear direction in terms of your priorities and expectations and to monitor those decisions.

We led by example. We were able to accomplish that by performing all the functions in a restaurant and showing our employees how we thought it should be done. We had a certain dedication and tenacity.

Whether you have one place or 100 places, you have to establish a structure, a culture, and a system, so you can be there or not and it still continues to work. It is hard to delegate and manage when you're not there. Although today it's still a problem in our companies to some extent, we're a lot better at it than we were when we started.

By 1973, we realized there were many people available in the industry with great talents. By bringing talent to the kitchen and to the front of the house, giving them the tools, the authority, and the incentive, we found we moved a lot quicker than we imagined possible.

When we started to attain a level of professionalism by bringing in the best of all departments, we really started to grow. This is something I wished we had learned a lot sooner. We thought we had to do everything ourselves in the beginning. We realized, however, that there are people who can do things as well, if not better than we can.

In trying to develop good working relationships, it is imperative to recognize that as the employer, you can't intimidate your employees. If they make a wrong decision, they are not failures. We had to understand that a flawed decision should be looked upon a part of the education process, something upon which employees can build and base their future decisions.

A second need was devising a plan to better organize our time. As we became more successful and continued to grow, Bert and I discovered we were increasingly being consumed by outside interests. Although we were flattered to serve on various boards and donate to civic, educational, and charitable foundations, we were gradually turning our time and energy away from where our main focus should have been, our own restaurants.

Presently, we have hired people within our companies to direct their energies toward these outside interests so we can spend more time running our operations. Among the most important decisions we make are not only what companies we want, but who is going to lead and manage them.

When we did expand, we developed five or six different theme restaurants, everything, including Chinese, steak houses, family operations, and fine dining. At one time, all of these seemed to be profitable. But as time passed, they became much harder to manage; and as concepts and tastes changed, we were spending a lot of time fixing one over here and changing one over there.

Regardless of how the events transpired with our different restaurants, the most important lesson we learned was the benefit of owning property rather than leasing. Owning property is a tremendous advantage, whereas leasing can become a liability.

The important lesson here for independent operators or any operators who seek long-term security is to be able to own your own properties. Some of the locations we lease today are ones we should have purchased.

Of the properties we owned, we were allowed in the long run to take the monies we saved and flow it back into our operations. We took the advantages we had in owning our property and gave it back to our customers through good value. Whereas with our leased properties, the rents continued to rise over the years, and we have had to pass that on to our customers.

Another great advantage of owning our properties is the increasing value due to appreciation. This benefits our financial statement and enables us to grow successfully by acquiring more property.

One of the benefits of owning your property is that you have a chance of getting out what you put into the restaurant when customers demand change and remodeling becomes a necessity. It's much easier to put substantial investment into your own property rather than in leased property.

For a lot of restaurateurs who are independent operators, owning their building becomes their greatest asset. When they get ready to retire, they keep the land and lease the restaurant which results in a strong equity base. Otherwise, some restaurateurs who have their entire life savings in the restaurant have had to walk away from the business after 25 years when the rent becomes prohibitive. A key decision early in an operator's business plan is whether or not to try to acquire as much property as possible.

Based on my experience, the restaurateur who wants to invest in a multi-unit concept should establish one theme, dedicate all of his or her energies to that theme, fine tune it, and then move on with it. You have a better chance of success, it's easier for management, and growth will be realized quicker. There's no doubt in my mind we had a lot of fun developing multi-themes and various menus, but it became a handicap as time went on. As we look back, it wasn't the prudent way to grow.

Leadership, however, isn't about trying to be perfect. It's about trying to set an example in all circumstances. There's an old saying: "A man who says he never had a chance, never took a chance." With leadership, you have to accept some decisions that aren't necessarily perfect. If there is one word in the English language I respect and treasure, it is *courage*. You must have the courage to take chances, be innovative, and, most of all, give authority to people to implement change.

We enjoyed tremendous success from the outset. Sometimes with so much success coming so quickly, one can become careless and start preaching rather than listening. I firmly believe God gave us two ears so we can spend twice the time listening and one mouth to spend a lot less time speaking. When we learned it was critical to listen to our employees and customers more and dictate to them less, we wound up being even more successful.

Today, we still have the same entrepreneurial spirit and the courage to make decisions. You can't let failures cause such paranoia that you don't act anymore. You have to move forward.

We have a saying at The Sardine Factory: "If we made you feel at home, we made a million dollar mistake because you might as well stay at home. Our job is to make you feel better than at home." If we can't do that, we're going to be out of business.

I've approached this business as if it's opening night every night. The human touch and the love of the customer is the most important factor in fine dining. As Benjamin Franklin said, "The taste of the roast depends on the handshake of the host."

In retrospect, there are some things I would have done differently, but overall I look back at my career in the hospitality field and have to be proud of my accomplishment.

Contract Services —
Each Contract Is Unique

John R. Farquharson is President of ARASERVE, the foodservice division of ARA Services, Inc. headquartered in Philadelphia, Pennsylvania. He is the 1990-91 Vice President of the National Restaurant Association.

Question: What is the most creative idea you have ever experienced in the hospitality industry?

During the past thirty years, I have lived with my company in the heart of the most creative idea I've ever experienced . . . and, we have grown together. I realize that it is one of the business world's amazing examples of what can happen when creativity is coupled with a leader's courage and faith in his or her managers. Let me explain.

Usually, in our dining and hospitality world, a successful entrepreneur will envision and create a concept by thoroughly visualizing and assembling all the resources, menu items, procedures, policies, specifications, features, standards, building design, etc., of the prototype operation and then either franchise or add company owned stores in the near identical image of the vision.

The manager of one of these chain units is expected to adhere to the formula exactly. Then, if the site selection is adequate, the unit is probably successful and the chain grows and prospers. We can point to many great successes in our profession that followed that developmental path.

But, in the scenario in which I have been living, the entrepreneur didn't have an easily reproducible design concept or menu concept. What the original entrepreneur had was a *service concept* — the notion that success in managing the employee dining services for one client on a contractual basis could be replicated virtually anywhere in the world,

21

regardless of the uniqueness of each situation.

No formula or cookie cutter approach could work in such a business. That creative entrepreneur had to hire the right people, impart to them standards and values, and then have the courage to place total faith in those managers to apply those standards and values with judgement, skill, and flexibility and to provide each client company, college, or hospital with the innovative dining service needed and desired for its unique situation. The successful, creative entrepreneur must do all of this while maintaining the consistent excellence necessary to build a healthy, growing world class company.

That's contract dining service management — a complex, exciting, highly successful industry that has boomed in my lifetime because a handful of great leaders not only had the creative vision of the concept but also had the courage to place faith in their employees to make it work.

Creative leaders with courage and faith in people. That's a powerful combination! It's still working, it's still growing, and it's still successful.

Success Is Based On Ethics

Richard C. Conti is Senior Principal and National Chairman, Food Service Practice Group, for Laventhol & Horwath, a Cleveland, Ohio based public accounting and management consulting organization.

Question: What is the essence of success as you define and believe in it?

I believe the essence of success can be defined as a strong desire not to fail at anything you do. That motivating force, that drive to achieve, comes from the desire to make everything you do have a successful outcome. When you combine this line of thinking with strong business ethics, you are pushed toward successful endeavors and pushed away from failures.

In my opinion, successful people are more risk-oriented than risk-adverse. If you take a chance on doing something new, if you can smell success by focusing on an area where you see a need or an opportunity, attack that project; don't avoid it. The payoff is that not only is the project successful, but you will also be viewed as a winner. Your extra time and effort and willingness to take a risk will lead to recognition. The rewards can be endless as long as the risk-oriented opportunities you recognize are in fact opportunities.

Your demonstration of enthusiasm and dedication to your job brings with it another key factor needed for success. Because of these motivating qualities, your peers will want to work with you. Your supervisors will want you on their team, and it is likely that someone in upper management will take an interest in you. That person can become your mentor. A mentor seems to find those people who show that they have a genuine interest in their work. They, too, want you as part of their team because of your desire to achieve. A mentor will cultivate your

23

abilities and assist you with your professional and career development. A mentor will not only applaud your efforts but will also inform other senior management people about your accomplishments.

Now that you have been an integral part of a team, what often happens next is your transformation into becoming a leader. I think of a leader as someone who can set the direction and, through his or her dedication and sincere belief in a particular goal, can motivate others to accomplish that goal. You strive to make those around you *want* to achieve the goal versus telling them they *have* to achieve the goal because you are the boss. You get them genuinely excited about the goal. This is a good philosophy for an effective leader. Successful leaders have successful people on their team.

One idea that directly relates to the leadership theme is the concept that everybody is a peer. With this in mind, you can be a strong leader by demonstrating to your staff that you respect their opinions and that team work, not just the effort of one individual, will accomplish the goal. You have to grasp and incorporate the idea that nobody is better or worse than anyone else. Whether you are dealing one-on-one with a staff member or the president of your company, respect each equally and work with the same intensity and enthusiasm in each instance. Again, the concept of peers and teamwork go hand in hand. A success story involves a lot of people who work toward a goal, and remember that often you are successful because those around you have contributed to that success.

I believe that a successful person also has to gain a handle on business and ethics. When you combine this into business-ethics, you develop a business situation that you are comfortable with, one that does not involve manipulation but rather cooperation. Your desire to achieve will be brought to fruition once you can be honest with yourself and with others regarding your work ethics. Both you and your company will benefit from your ethical operations in business situations.

In summation, I believe that if you have the drive to be successful combined with the qualities it takes to be an achiever while focusing on a team approach, you will reach your goal.

Complementarity Between Family Interests And A Professional Career

Richard J. Harman is Chairman of Myron Green Cafeterias Company, Inc., headquartered in Kansas City, Kansas. He is a past president of the National Restaurant Association.

Question: What is the essence of success as you define and believe in it?

The essence of success has as many meanings as there are people to ponder it. One concept of success is to couple one's personal and family interests, dreams, and aspirations with a business or professional career that complement and fortify each other.

I believe that the hospitality industry is a perfect vehicle for the expression of our inner instincts. Hospitality gives us a stage to develop our lives to the greatest degree. It offers high public visibility, and the opportunities for creativity are boundless. It also offers public and industry service outlets which can develop leadership potential.

In hospitality, relationships with fellow workers are far more personal than is true with most occupations. Fellow workers cover a wide range of talent, educational achievement, motivation, and emotional needs. Similarly, your customers represent a challenge to you to win their loyal support and approval each time they enter your establishment. You attend to the multitude of details that have to be in place each day to insure customer satisfaction.

Hospitality offers a unique opportunity to interact with people from all walks of life. I think hospitality operators earn an informal Ph.D. in psychology each day they set foot in their units.

What does all this mean to a restaurateur? It means there is an open-ended opportunity to develop our personality, reasoning ability, evaluative processes, leadership, communication, style, appreciation for people and their contributions, and a confidence to be able to manage a wide range of responsibilities.

When we are young, we begin to realize that there are opportunities to shape our degree of enjoyment, satisfaction, and feeling of worth from our participation in the world around us. For most of us, there is a strong desire to be involved in the world around us. We then recognize that certain people in our orbits are influencing what is happening. In many instances, there might be strong emotional, physical, and mental competition where events are being shaped. This can lead to moments of great satisfaction when something worthwhile has been achieved.

It soon becomes clear that the more one challenges oneself to become involved in a wide range of leadership roles, the greater the joys of success or the greater the aches of failure. No risk, no rewards, and no rewards can lead to a dull life.

At some juncture in time, we learn or we're taught by hard experience to limit endeavors outside our field of activity. Experience is a marvelous teacher focusing our thoughts.

As careers develop, meetings can occupy a great deal of time. If a meeting is worth going to, you should actively participate in it. Another belief of mine is: If an organization or group is going to occupy your time and thoughts, you should be willing to seek and assume leadership and responsibility.

As you build your organization around you and you are involved in many other activities, frustrations obviously can be a serious problem. Matching people who find satisfaction with your style of leadership is a major challenge because the measure of success does not always rank making money as a top personal priority. This can place enormous stress on building an organization, particularly when profits aren't flowing freely.

One thing I learned early in my career: If you give volunteer organizations your best leadership and effort you move up the ladder of responsibility rapidly. We have faced great challenges in trade, civic, public, and other activities, yet these activities may alter our business and financial involvement.

Family life also plays a strong role in shaping success. One's spouse needs to be totally supportive of your activities. Children grow up rapidly and we can unwittingly pay a high price for having a deep commitment to a wide range of activities. Problems can develop when one assumes leadership roles in outside activities. In working with many people in volunteer activities, one can develop a strong thirst for the excitement of challenge that can quickly sap your ability to give the proper attention (at the necessary times) to your family, friends, community, church, and business. This volunteerism needs to be managed carefully and priorities need to be balanced and continually reviewed.

Your satisfaction grows when members of your family or your organization become involved in leadership roles that benefit mankind. Some of the most meaningful moments come when family members reinforce each other's activities.

It is fortunate to learn early in life that humor plays a very important role in diffusing stress. A positive outlook is a must for your mental and physical health. Not taking yourself too seriously is a great release valve. Poking fun and laughing at yourself can be effective in many situations.

There may be times when you fail to reach an important goal. This can be a time for reassessment. You can roll with the punch, get up from the dust, and go on to new challenges. Conversely, you can pup your tent and begrudge your failures, nothing good comes from that.

Some of your greatest opportunities may emerge after a severe setback. Character can grow under severe pressures. In perspective, there are many times you can quit or decide striving for a particular goal is not worth the price. Don't give up. A withdrawal is not a retreat if you come back or attack a different flank.

In my nearly 60 years, the hospitality industry has gone through increasingly rapid changes. There are vast areas in which I have no experience or knowledge. Then I realize, the most important thing we as individuals can do is participate in helping to develop an industry and a society in which increasing numbers of persons are encouraged to give their best thoughts and leadership in their areas of expertise. Our hope for now and for the future is to play a part in encouraging a higher percentage of our citizens to be active participants by giving meaning to their leadership roles. We all must be strong enough to accept challenge, as well as defeat.

My telescope to the future indicates we have come dangerously close to destroying many of our freedoms by wanting too much for ourselves without regard to the long-range price. The hospitality industry has emerged as a strong industry with immense potential to influence the direction of our nation. Never has the need been greater for leaders to take on more responsibilities and to help shape public policies.

Hospitality industry leaders clearly have the opportunity and incentive to play a greater role in national, political, economic, and social life. We can and should have a strong role in influencing the third century of the American Way of Life.

Success Is Not A 100 Yard Dash

James M. Irwin is President and Chief Executive Officer of Emco Foodservice Systems (formerly CODE, Inc.), a major foodservice industry distribution firm headquartered in Pittsburgh, Pennsylvania. He is a member of the Foodservice Distribution Hall of Fame.

Question: What is the essence of success as you define and believe in it?

One of the formal definitions for success is "exceptional performance and achievement." I believe this statement pretty well defines what success is, but I would add a time period to it. I'd say success is exceptional performance and achievement on a consistent basis over a period of time.

I feel it is also necessary to define achievement when addressing success. I see achievement as an act of accomplishment of something noteworthy. Taking these two thoughts into consideration, I view success in a number of ways.

First of all, it is using your God-given talents and abilities to maximize your potential.

I have always believed that the vast majority of people do not work to the full potential of their capabilities. Many are not willing to pay the price for success, yet do not realize the rewards far outweigh the costs. Many people follow a path of "least resistance" that limits their ability to exercise their full potential.

As it pertains to business and one's vocation, success to me is many things. It is achieving a leadership position in one's field of endeavor. It is running a stable and profitable business; however, I do not think of success strictly in terms of profit and loss results. It is the motivation and development of people. It is sharing your knowledge and experience with the people you train. I do not think a person is successful if they do not develop others to go on to achieve success.

Success is also overcoming challenges. Every individual in business, sooner or later, runs into adversity. Success is dealing with adversity and overcoming it. It is being at one's best when the chips are on the line. It is taking negatives and turning them into positives on a consistent basis. A successful person will lead with an authority earned by integrity and not compromise ethics or morals for financial gain or position.

Success is adjusting to change and meeting each challenge as it occurs. Really successful people take on challenges; they don't run or hide from them. They become problem preventers and problem solvers and take satisfaction in this type of achievement.

In business, economic goals have to be met to achieve financial success, but reaching that goal, in my opinion, does not mean you are totally successful. It is all of the things I have already mentioned and many more.

Successful persons earn the respect of their peers. They give something back to the industry that is good to them. They are instrumental in the development of other people. They become a mentor to others along the way.

Successful people also strive to be better performers. They learn as much from a lost sale or missed opportunity in business as they do from successful missions. They are never satisfied with their own performance. There must be dedication and drive to reach greater heights of performance.

Successful people will take what they've learned from business and carry it over into their personal lives whether it be a partner in marriage, a parent to children, or a good friend to others. To them, the *process* of achieving success is equally as, if not more, important than the end result.

I've often asked myself what constitutes success. There are a few words that come to my mind, all synonyms with one another. Persistence, determination, "stick-to-it-iveness."

Success is reaching goals you set in a worthy manner. Goals must be set high but be obtainable. You must always be reaching. To achieve success you must work hard, you must work smart.

There is no easy way. The road to success is paved with stumbling blocks. How well you handle each stumbling block will determine the measure of success one achieves. Many successful people have early failures that are humbling and character building. Each person in business starts out with some skills and some weaknesses. The successful person overcomes the weakness and develops skills in those areas that weren't natural or inbred. One develops tenacity and perseverance as he or she climbs the ladder to success.

As it pertains to business, success is not achieved in days, weeks, months, or even a few years, but over a period of time.

Successful business people are not the 100 yard dash sprinters; they are the marathon runners.

Marathon runners endure pain along the way; at times they endure fatigue and discouragement, but they don't give up. They keep their minds on their objective and an eye on the finish line! They don't get off course, they maintain singleness of purpose toward the goal. This same rule applies in business.

To be perceived and recognized as a leader and as a successful person by one's peers is one of the highest compliments that an individual can receive.

Ask The Right Questions

Charles P. "Buzz" McCormick, Jr. is Chairman of the Board and Chief Executive Officer of McCormick & Company, Inc., an international producer of seasonings, flavorings and specialty foods.

Question: What is the essence of success as you define and believe in it?

I believe success is often based on a knack for asking the right questions at the right time to the right people.

One of the things my father, C.P. McCormick, believed in was asking the right questions; in fact, the whole participative management system we call "Multiple Management" is based on this idea.

My father believed that, "the person on the job is often best able to say how that job ought to be done." Many managements today forget to ask the people best able to answer their questions for ideas about how to improve quality, how to be innovative, how to get better efficiency. They forget to ask their own employees, those who are actually charged with the responsibility of doing the job everyday.

My father helped McCormick believe, and many other companies too, that there is *powerful*, untapped potential in people. He felt we ought to find ways to turn on that potential by asking the people who work for us for their help and their best ideas and then reward them with proper recognition.

Three years ago when I was named Chief Executive Officer of the company one of the very first things I did was send a memo to all of our management and sales employees. In essence, I asked them to tell me informally what they thought we ought to do to make McCormick an even more successful, dynamic, and innovative company.

Dolores, my secretary, and I were swamped. Our employees' response was even greater than we had hoped for but not entirely unexpected because our basic management philosophy is based on a belief in the worth of the individual, "the power of people."

But we don't merely say we believe in people, as some companies do. We live this belief by doing everything we can to encourage the enthusiastic participation of all our employees toward making us a total quality company.

Last year the Executive Committee and I decided that the primary mission of the Company was to expand our worldwide leadership position in the seasoning and flavoring markets and thus increase overall value for our shareholders.

My memo asked for the participation and the focus of everyone toward finding the best ways to accomplish this mission.

Now you must undersetand that asking for participation at McCormick is not the same thing as it may be at other companies. Our people participate — I mean they really participate! This stems from the basic multiple management system we pioneered in 1932.

Back then someone nicknamed it "management by many" or "50 heads are better than one." We find that when we've got everyone on board and enthusiastic to move ahead that they're properly motivated, not merely driven by decisions made upstairs.

It's our own people who make the difference and they are the ones who can make things happen if we can just remember to ask the right questions. As a new CEO, it was amazing to me that after reviewing the responses to my employee memo how focused my own vision for the company's future became.

Obviously our employees also liked being asked for their participation, and obviously our reputation for employee participation was once again in evidence.

It's this philosophy of individual worth and recognition that creates the successful sense of teamwork at McCormick. We work at things together. Everyone gets to participate in creating our success.

I believe this heritage of participation, teamwork, and shared accomplishment is one of the basic reasons for our continued success and growth into a billion dollar organization.

Success Has A Future Perspective

Ferdinand Metz (MBA), Certified Master Chef, is President of the Culinary Institute of America headquartered in Hyde Park, New York. He is a trustee of the U.S. Culinary Team Foundation and is a former manager of the U.S. Culinary Team.

Question: What is the essence of success as you define and believe in it?

To be successful, you must possess exemplary leadership qualities. You must be a fair manager, an inspiring motivator, and, most of all, a diplomat when dealing with people. These leadership qualities alone, however, do not ensure success. You must also have a good deal of expertise in your field. This knowledge, combined with personal qualities, will allow you to make a significant contribution to your chosen profession.

It is important to understand that exemplary leadership qualities and expertise in your field must then again be combined with a burning desire to succeed. Knowledge, no matter how easily acquired, must be applied vigorously. You must be able to accept criticism and learn from it. Your expertise will be built on a firm foundation of fundamental concepts, learned not only through your education but also through your daily experience. You must always be ready to begin anew, improving your abilities, and continually renewing your commitment to excellence.

Your expertise will also present you with insights into the industry's history, the trends of today, and the outlook for tomorrow, allowing you further impact upon the growth of your industry. For example, during the early part of this decade, a group of faculty members and I saw a need for incorporating the principles of nutrition into the curriculum at The Culinary Institute of America. This idea initially was received with skepticism, but we felt very strongly that nutrition would be a future demand made upon the foodservice industry by the public. We established St. Andrew's Cafe, a student-staffed restaurant that serves "good food that is good for you." The concept was so successful and its acceptance so widespread throughout the industry that today the school has opened a three million dollar Nutrition Center.

To be a successful leader, you must determine what it is you believe in and become totally committed to it. Let your beliefs become your passion, a driving force that excites you and motivates you to accomplish great things within the industry.

Once you have established this belief or mission, put your motivation to work in a pragmatic and logical manner. Set deadlines and goals for yourself in the present and for 20 years down the road. Develop a plan of activities that will result in tangible, beneficial results.

As you plan your strategies for achieving your goals allow for a bit of flexibility to accommodate delays, change of lifestyle, and other factors that may throw your plan off schedule. Be able to adapt, but never lose sight of your ultimate goals.

When your plan is complete, share your perceptions for the future with your peers in the industry, and determine whether or not they agree with your vision. Listening to the opinions and insights of other people will be a crucial factor in reaching your goals for the future.

Once you are secure with your goals, surround yourself with knowledgeable people who share your basic philosophy, but who will also share their expertise and opinions with you. Build a team that will work towards a common objective. Lead by example. Always be willing to do what you will ask others to do. They will respect you for this.

Be patient; success is not achieved overnight. Don't allow yourself to become consumed by your goal. Maintain a sense of balance, allowing yourself involvement in both physical and mental activities at work and outside the workplace.

It may be beneficial to establish subgoals that you can realize within a certain period of time. This will allow you some immediate gratification and will help you maintain a fairly clear perspective of the future.

As you travel the road to success, take time to re-analyze your goals. Are they still realistic and attainable? Do your present strategies need minor modification or a total overhaul? Does your goal still coincide with the demands and needs of your industry? If not, what can you do to ensure your future success? Reassessment of career goals is a continual process. You must constantly monitor your environment to measure the impact of your actions, keep in constant touch with industry leaders, and listen to what they are saying.

Remember that success means different things to different people. Some can be satisfied with the partial completion of their goal. Others must see it through to its total conclusion. You will know you have achieved ultimate success when your goal has made a significant impact on your industry, is beneficial to others, will continue to impact upon the industry years into the future, and, most importantly, has given you a great deal of personal satisfaction. That is the essence of success.

Make Excellence A Habit

Patrick L. O'Malley is Chairman Emeritus of Canteen Company which he joined in 1962 following a 28-year business career with the Coca-Cola Company. He is past President of the National Restaurant Association.

Question: What is the essence of success as you define and believe in it?

In a business career that has spanned 50 years, I've held, essentially, two jobs. For nearly 30 years, from 1933 to 1961, I was associated in a variety of management positions with the Coca-Cola Company. For the next 20 years, I headed Canteen Corporation, and since my retirement have held an emeritus post with Canteen.

I can scarcely count the chairmanships, trusteeships, directorships, and other posts that entered my life during these 50 years, positions which occupy my time as much with community affairs as with business. I've always felt that these positions represent a pretty good scorecard of business success. If the Class D Baseball Club in Oshkosh, Wisconsin, thought I could help them keep their franchise and improve their game, they must have figured I knew how to go about promotion and marketing which I was supposed to be doing in business.

If the National Restaurant Association, the National Automatic Merchandising Association, and other organizations wanted me at their helms, I must have given my own company the kind of leadership that drew their attention and admiration.

In other words, a number of community organizations turned to me as a businessman successful in my own field and in the expectation that I could help them reach their goals as well. That's a measure of success I have long accepted as valid.

In my experience as a corporate executive, I was a people person dedicated to service, always trying to make things happen, running toward problems — not away from them, getting things done through people, making everyone's job important, pushing hard for perfection, setting the best possible example, and always finding time to do the necessary and reserving time for community service. As a CEO, I found ways to leverage the experience gained from innovative, imaginative, creative, and financial management within a business environment based on being people sensitive.

The genesis of achievement is in one place and one place only; achievement begins with ourselves. It begins with the spark of desire to get the job done. I found that before the spark of desire can be nurtured into the fire of achievement, I had to eliminate some of the dampening influences that tended to make this spark of desire sputter and fail. I had to do away with my own limp wristed cynicism that so often served as a cloak to hide my willingness to make significant decisions that frequently were a measure of the company's success.

Leadership, as an underpinning of success, seems to be a matter of doing the job at hand with all the energy required with all your resources being used efficiently. It means getting the right people in the right place for the job they will be committed to achieve. It means managing human resources, motivating your colleagues and employees, directing them skillfully, providing adequate training, establishing reporting relationships, getting to understand them and communicating with them, giving them the responsibility and the authority to complete their mission and following up to make sure that the authority has not been mishandled.

It is also important to take risks to succeed — not to act rashly, but to weigh the factors that will contribute to your reaching a given goal and then to act on your decision.

If you fear taking risks, recognize it and replace it with love of your challenge. Leaders must have vision. Without vision, people stagnate.

In so many decisions it is not merely a matter of just making an executive decision. You have to make it work: The board of directors needs persuasion, shareholders must be kept satisfied, the sales force properly motivated, and the rest of the work force stimulated — all to insure that you've reduced the risk you are taking to an acceptable level, thus giving yourself an optimum chance to succeed in making proper use of resources and management.

Leadership involves a process that increases organizational effectiveness and efficiency by being sure that the effort of employees is directed to the kind of activities that will ensure quality, cost control, and the continuing enlargement of the overall scope of business.

Success implies recognition, but it first demands excellence. My dad always told me from the time I went out at age seven to earn money shining shoes, "Whatever you do, you must do it well," and my nickel shoeshines were good enough that they frequently earned me a ten-cent tip.

And the way to excellent performance? It takes study, hard work, continued learning about the job, and implementation of the tasks you are assigned. I've found in recent years that I can often predict which member of a group of candidates will succeed by watching someone who may not have the college degree or the MBA or the computer skills, but who is absolutely determined to educate himself or herself. Often that person will be the first to reach the goal. Excellence has to become a habit if you are going to set a pattern for success.

Integrity is an equally significant part of it, and success requires an unquestioned honesty in what you are trying to accomplish. Whether a businessperson approaches success from developing the product, tallying its sales, mapping a marketing program, maintaining the quality of its advertising, or controlling the finances that enable the company to grow, this underlying honesty is absolutely necessary. It's basic to the success of any product, service, or program.

Leadership requires constant vigilance. Operational strategies, organizational structure, product mix, cost analysis, competition, field support, levels of management, technology, and profitability are all subject to change, and my experience suggests the leader who takes a systematic approach to change will build the best mousetrap. Given those factors, the task of leadership becomes a matter of communicating with the people around you: Do those who get their direction from you feel it's a two-way street? That you care about their response? That you want their respect and give them yours? These are important factors no matter how technically advanced a job may seem. I want my people to be the best that they can be as this requires me to be the best that I can be. It's people who carry out the instructions and take pride in contributing to the company's success.

How you measure it, how you define it, success is certainly a personal judgment.

I think each of us knows the feeling that success generates — we're proud, we're eager to repeat. Quite often, the successful person is looking for new fields to conquer. Perhaps that's part of the reason all those civic organizations are looking for the busiest person in their communities; if an executive's company is doing well, there's an appetite for success and for another challenge.

One benefit is that the local hospital, college or university, or home rule commission achieves a quality of leadership they couldn't otherwise afford, and that reflects the best in the community. That's part of a businessperson's responsibility, and there surely is a concomitant benefit to one's business through winning the respect of the community and of other businesses for this type of activity. Another aspect of success is that it allows you to exercise your judgment more freely than you might do otherwise, to give more latitude to young talent who can bring vigor to your company. It allows you to encourage the imagination that can be a generator of new business methods, new products, or new marketing approaches. It even enables you to dedicate your career to worthwhile efforts so that you remain productive as long as you love the work. For many a successful person, that's for as long as you live and it makes living worthwhile.

Assessing Executives:
Look For Vision And Implementation

Richard P. Mayer is a former Chairman and Chief Executive Officer, Kentucky Fried Chicken of Louisville, Kentucky, one of the nation's largest quick service chains. In 1989, he joined General Foods Corporation as President.

Question: What key qualities and values do you look for in assessing management talent?

A wise man once said, "Experience is a hard teacher. It gives the test first, and then you learn the lesson." Given those cruel facts, the recruitment and retention of able managers who know the "lessons" is a necessity of modern business.

For purposes of this discussion, my focus is on assessing executive talent and identifying the skills individuals need to prosper and grow for the benefit of oneself and the company. Such assessment is one of the management's most powerful levers in moving the business forward and creating the bench strength all companies must have to sustain and fortify themselves.

But it is nearly impossible to judge people accurately by either rigid or abstract measures alone. That's especially true when you have not had a first hand association with an individual. So when evaluating the talent and potential of managers, I try to apply a number of rather broad-ranging guidelines, and I often seek the opinions of others to cross-check my readings or observations.

Having appropriate education and technical skills for the job are a given, of course. But more often than not, the qualities and values that determine a manager's long term effectiveness and achievement are found beyond those basic prerequisites.

Among the key traits and factors that I look for are: established personal goals, the drive and ambition to attain those goals (tempered and strengthened with integrity), proven analytical and communications skills, superior interpersonal capabilities, a sense of humor, an awareness and appreciation of the world beyond his or her business speciality, receptivity to ideas (no matter the source), and finally, a genuine, deep commitment to growth and profitability of the business.

That sounds a bit like a profile for Superman or Wonder Woman. But it's really only a set of guidelines. No one expects to find a "perfect 10" in any or all of these qualities. That would be unrealistic. Yet it is realistic to expect to find something more than a trace of these factors in people — whether they are potential new employees starting at the lower rungs or candidates for top positions of leadership. And it's important to look carefully at each individual to unearth the person's capacity for enhancing these traits through coaching, experience, and self-development.

All that is well and good, but it raises the question, "How do you go about effectively and consistently identifying the best people?" The answer lies in a two-phased process of selection and executive development.

The second phase, the developmental process, is relatively easy if you have selected the right people in the first place. The trick is to use a selection process that elicits solid indications of the presence (or lack) of the key traits you desire.

An important element of such interviewing and evaluation is to make sure that, in turn, the candidate gets a clear picture of your organization's culture, its mission, operating style, values, and positioning. After all, no one can make a full commitment to a company without knowing where it's going and what it stands for.

The techniques of interviewing are pretty standard across American business and the restaurant industry with tailoring, of course, to fit a given company's situation. In the area of creativity and innovation, the candidate is likely to be asked to describe the conditions under which his or her best creative thinking has been conducted. Typically, this is followed by extensive discussion of how the individual's ideas have been implemented by an employer.

Similarly, strong indications of traits and skills such as: drive and ambition; capability of handling complexity; strategic thinking; staffing and people development; persuasiveness, and maturity can be gleaned from wide-ranging, but specific discussion of personal goals and accomplishments.

Even leadership qualities can be ascertained to a fairly accurate degree this way. Leaders, for example, tend to think and talk about matters beyond the horizon of quarterly or annual operating concerns. They clearly see the breadth of the environment, internal and external, and the strength of their vision and personalities often influences people beyond the boundaries of the organization chart or job description.

Once you have determined the qualities you seek in executives, can you rely solely on a thorough, even exhaustive, interviewing program to achieve your goals? Clearly, the interview process (bolstered by thorough background checks) is a primary tool of executive assessment — especially in the hiring phase. But, the interview is not enough when considering internal candidates for promotion to top management positions. That assessment must include a careful review of each candidate's track record in two key measurements of effective leadership: vision and organizational implementation.

Starting with vision, the operative question that must be answered is, "Has this person demonstrated a capability of setting direction to change and enhance the future of the company?" Here, one looks for job performance that shows: 1) the individual visualized what could and should have been done; 2) the individual developed a strategy to achieve the vision that embraced existing organizational and environmental factors and took into account trends and probable resulting changes over the planning horizon.

Secondly, it's important to assess the person's past performance in building an organization or network to implement the vision. Key measurements in this area include winning the support of the organization's power structure, developing strong relationships throughout the company to ensure cooperation and compliance with the strategy, and creating a lead group which is fully committed to achieving the vision on schedule and within budget.

Summing up, I believe a plan is necessary to assure success and consistency in evaluating management talent. Analyze the needs of your business. Write down the qualities and leadership skills you need to put your company ahead of the rest. And stick to them when you assess people for jobs and promotions. The great management expert, Peter Drucker, said, "Long-range planning does not deal with future decisions, but with the future of present decisions." The truth of that statement is never more evident that when selecting today's and tomorrow's management team.

Be Your Own Most Demanding Customer

Ray L. Danner is former Chairman and Chief Executive of Shoney's Inc., a diversified foodservice operator headquartered in Nashville, Tennessee. He is Senior Chairman and CEO but is retired from active duty with Shoney's.

Question: What is the most creative idea you have ever experienced in the hospitality industry?

I don't think of myself as being particularly creative. My specialty has been as an innovator, making things happen. For example, I have now completed 31 years in the food industry. I could see, through the success of McDonald's and other small independent drive-in creations, eating out would become a growth industry.

After making the commitment to join the food industry, I have then and forever since used myself as the most critical and demanding customer who could possibly visit one of our units. From that self-recognition of my talent, my strongest points are that I can hire, train, and motivate all the personnel necessary to be successful in what is today a mature industry.

My personal rewards in our company's success are due to the thousands of employees I have influenced throughout the years, always stressing that the customer is our ULTIMATE BOSS. To continue to succeed we will need to be constantly sensitive, making sure we stay the innovators we are to the benefit and satisfaction of our customers.

The Name Is Important

Martin L. Horn, Jr. is President of Martin L. Horn Associates, Inc., agents, brokers and consultants to the hospitality industry, located in Tequesta, Florida. Over the past 30 years he has owned and operated several types of foodservice operations in New Jersey and Florida. He is a past president of the National Restaurant Association.

Question: What is the most creative idea you have ever experienced in the hospitality industry?

Having spent over a third of a century in the restaurant business, I thought that this would be an easy question to answer. After giving it considerable thought, however, I discovered how complex it can be.

At the outset let me say that if I have any creative instincts or an ability to spot creativity, I derived it from my father who was one of the true and great natural restaurateurs. When I say natural, I mean he had a native instinct for creating what people wanted and expected when they visited a restaurant. He provided value priced quality food with attentive service in physically and psychologically comfortable surroundings. He didn't go to school to learn how to do this; he just possessed those basic instincts and was able to pass on to others his talent for innovation and inspiration.

I believe that creativity comes from the accumulation of experience of what we see, who we talk to, where we go, what we read about, and what we gather from the remarks of others. A lot of the good ideas we implemented took root in the remarks and suggestions of our employees and our customers with whom we have always had good, honest relationships. We would alter ideas, refine them, experiment with them, make other alterations, and then stay with them or discard them. Creativity is a process, not a product — a concept that leads me to describe our most creative experience, our newest restaurant.

For years I have been friends with the former great New York Giants running back Alex Webster. When we sold our New Jersey operations in 1988 and moved to Florida, Alex happened to be doing public relations work for a foodservice firm. In the course of things we became aware of a restaurant and club that was for sale, which bore a striking resemblance to a New York steak house. We decided to construct a little bit of New York in southern Florida.

All restaurant concepts begin with a relationship between the market sought and the menu offered, conditioned by economic considerations. We developed popular entrées (for our market) which require minimal pre-preparation and storage, and that are low in waste and spoilage potential. Value is the byword we live by in making pricing decisions. We wanted the atmosphere to be casual, but not overly relaxed; dignified, not common. The decor had to be eye appealing and hold continuing interest. Furniture and fixtures are part of that, but Alex Webster had a great collection of sports photos and memorabilia which we incorporated into the design. We bought helmet replicas of the 26 teams in the National Football League and hung color photos of sports stars we knew were in the area or would be likely to visit the area. About half of the pictures we installed have now been personally autographed. We installed five television sets for reviewing sports events and videotapes of memorable games and plays.

Determining the right name took a little thought. We knew we wanted to capitalize on Alex's name, but we didn't want to put "sports" in the name since that might attract a broader market than we were targeting. We considered "Alex Webster's New York Steakhouse" but thought "Steakhouse" might be too product specific, and "New York" might not necessarily attract people from other regions of the country. Always remember, the name is usually the first thing that draws an image in the mind of a potential customer. We settled on "Alex Webster's Restaurant and Bar." We hired a manager — actually took him in as a third partner — who is also a former pro football player and who has had considerable restaurant management experience.

A restaurant also has to have a personality of its own, and that can only be implemented by its staff. It took a little time to put together the team we wanted to serve our patrons, but we're there.

Employee recruitment, selection, training and retention all take a lot of time and effort, but they are the cornerstone of a good restaurant operation. The first year of operation exceeded our expectations in all respects.

In summation, the name is important in attracting the patron. The atmosphere, the attention of the staff, and the personality of the restaurant are important in drawing the patron back. The most important ingredient, however, is the food on the plate.

As for the most creative idea I've ever experienced — it will be the next one.

Combine Forces For Creative Solutions

James F. Murphy is Chairman of Hiram Walker-Allied Vintners, Inc., Detroit, Michigan, a position he assumed after 37 years of service with the firm. He is a trustee of the National Commission Against Drunk Driving.

Question: What is the most creative idea you have ever experienced in the hospitality industry?

"Good ideas" abound within an atmosphere of creativity and innovation. They flourish and grow to maturity when given the breath of life by a progressive management and a responding public.

And these "good ideas" become even "better ideas" when they are generated as a response and solution to an identified problem — whether large or small, local or national, broad or specific.

A common problem that both the foodservice industry and our alcoholic beverage industry must face is the continuing pressure being exerted by outside forces affecting the consumption of alcohol.

One of the major issues confronting our industry is the emergence of a worldwide anti-alcohol movement. The forces are pervasive in their political and organization lobbying within all levels of government and professional organizations. Until recently the activities were confined largely to the United States and the United Kingdom; but consistent with other trends, this issue is quickly becoming a global one.

As a major U.S. and international wines and spirits organization, Hiram Walker-Allied Vintners is obviously deeply concerned and involved. The foodservice industry also continues to be seriously affected. And, it makes good, economic sense that we, the wine and spirits industry, work along with the foodservice industry in response to our common problem which, if left without creative resolve, could have devastating results for both of us.

These problems began to surface in the early and mid-1980's, forcing dramatic changes on the licensed foodservice operator and the alcohol beverage supplier. We had previously enjoyed a decade of relative calm when the ratio of liquor to food and resulting profit continued to grow. Suddenly, profit and even survival pressures increased as a result of declining alcohol beverage sales. We were faced with burgeoning liability insurance rates and restrictive legislation of all kinds. Added to this is the aging of America, which created changes in guest priorities, preferences and lifestyles. All of this has been compounded by the external alcohol awareness pressures we are facing today.

This is clearly the time for responsible operators and suppliers to emerge and join together with creative ideas which will not only restore public confidence but also place the service of alcoholic beverages in its proper perspective within the hospitality industry. The answer is not to look toward making alcohol more expensive or difficult to buy, or to manipulate consumers with the false conviction that alcohol is hazardous to health. The answer, of course, is to encourage sensible consumption levels. This does not come from overly repressive, restrictive measures, but from sound, comprehensive educational methods.

Mankind has long enjoyed the pleasures of beers, wines, and spirits to relieve the fatigue of labor, for relaxation from stress, for social pleasures, and to stimulate a healthy appetite. Its use by the majority does not lead to either problems of health or social disorder. I stress that it is not unlike any other product which, if excessively abused, has its downside.

We are responding. This response is coming from many directions: from independent to multi-unit operations, from the associations which bind them together, and from those of us within the wine and spirits industry.

In combating this major threat there have been many problem solving "better ideas" and it is impossible for me to identify any single one that clearly stands out above all others. So, I would prefer, instead, to identify a collection of "better ideas" that have been generated by these two industries.

Alcohol Awareness Training programs for operators and servers have emerged from a variety of responsible sponsors. Operators and suppliers are responding with a variety of designated driver and transportation programs. As responsible suppliers, training programs have been instituted to make our representatives more sensitive to the needs of the industry. We are training our sales force to be professionals when dealing with account opportunities and responsible product usage.

Other creative ideas stemmed from a need; operators felt a responsibility to replace excessive multiple drink promotion programs. As an alternative, many are now featuring more profitable, premium brands. A larger selection of premium wines by the glass are also showing new profit opportunities as well. We have joined foodservice operators in the promotion of profitable, lower alcohol, speciality, and signature drinks.

Operator profits are being enhanced with a variety of dessert drink specialties where the moderation theme is promoted.

With guests drinking less but more elegantly, cocktails are once again being served as a result of programs created by establishments such as The Rainbow Room in New York. The Canadian Club "Return to Elegance" program is one example of such a promotion, encouraging the return to traditional cocktail enjoyment.

Over the years we have sponsored hospitality management scholarships to numerous universities throughout the United States. I'm proud to say that we are a major supporter of the Cornell University's School of Hotel Administration. An important link between beverage producers, distributors, and on-premise accounts in the hospitality industry, our sponsorship is designated to the Vance A. Christian Beverage Management Center and specifically to the Hiram Walker-Allied Vintners Management Center Bar.

This one-of-a-kind teaching facility is dedicated to the in-depth study of current issues affecting the beverage industry and is used by students and alumni, as well as the hospitality and beverage industry. Through this partnership we are sharing the interests of the school and the hospitality industry, and providing an understanding of the beverage industry through product knowledge and sound, responsible management principles.

I am confident that through this sponsorship we are helping to ensure our collective future. For it is these students and those in other programs who will become our next generation of restaurant owners, food and beverage directors, and tomorrow's corporate executives of companies within the food and beverage industry. It is to them that we must look for future creative ideas and sound leadership.

Indeed, the burden of responsible leadership has clearly been placed upon the shoulders of the hospitality industry. And, as part of that industry, we have responded to the challenges of the 80's, and will continue to do so in the 90's and beyond. The lesson that we all must learn is that these challenges will continue, and we must counter and contain them with creative ideas — ideas which will emerge from an atmosphere created by responsible leadership.

The Industry Owes Its Growth To Franchising

Ronald N. Paul is President of Technomic, Inc., a Chicago based research, marketing, and business consulting organization with broad experience in the food and foodservice industries.

Question: What is the most creative idea you have ever experienced in the hospitality industry?

After giving the subject of "the most creative idea in hospitality" considerable thought, it became obvious in my mind that the most creative, major idea that has impacted on the industry is the concept of franchising.

At first blush, it is hard to think about franchising as an idea since it so often is wrapped up in legalese and has become an accepted way of doing business.

While franchising in terms of licensing a product or trade name has been around for a long time as a business tool, its usage was limited to automotive dealers, gasoline service stations, and soft drink bottlers. On the other hand, the development of what is referred to as business format franchising is of more recent vintage having had its origins in the pre-depression era, with hospitality chains such as Howard Johnson's and A&W being the early pioneers.

When one gets closer to the hospitality industry and its two major components, restaurants and lodging, the importance of franchising can be seen. At the current time, the importance of franchising in the economy and in the hospitality industry can be noted by a quick review of the following tables:

FRANCHISING IN THE ECONOMY
1989

- 2,200 Firms
- In Excess of 500,000 Outlets
- Sales of Nearly $700 Billion
- 7,000,000 Employed

SOURCE: U.S. Department of Commerce

FRANCHISING IN THE LODGING
AND RESTAURANT INDUSTRIES
1989 ESTIMATES

Restaurant Industry - Franchised Businesses

Sales	$64 Billion
Number of Establishments	91,000
Employed	2,700,000
Sales Growth 1988/1987	11.2%
Unit Growth	9.9%

Lodging Industry — Franchised Businesses

Sales	$20 Billion
Number of Establishments	10,400
Employed	650,000
Sales Growth 1988/1987	11.0%
Unit Growth	11.6%

SOURCE: U.S. Department of Commerce

The success of the largest restaurant chain, McDonald's, can in many ways be traced to Ray Kroc's early decision to utilize the franchise system for expanding the distribution of his units. As told in his autobiography, when he was contemplating franchising he was fortunate enough to run into Harry Sonneborn who was a Vice President with Tastee Freeze. As Ray stated,

> "In the first place, I had to mobilize my franchise sales and start generating some cash flow. Secondly, I was in the field by myself at the moment, but I knew that others would soon be jumping in to compete, and I wanted to take full advantage of my head start . . ."
>
> "One of the basic decisions I made in this period affected the heart of my franchise system and how it would develop. It was that the corporation was not going to get involved in being a supplier for its operators. My belief was that I had to help the individual operator succeed in every way I could. His success would insure my success. But I couldn't do that and, at the same time, treat him as a customer."

Ray Kroc's recognition of the effectiveness of franchising and franchising rights led directly to McDonald's strong position in both the hamburger segment as well as the entire fast food industry. As evidence of this leadership, by early 1989 the McDonald's U.S. system had grown to in excess of 10,500 restaurants and enjoyed systemwide sales on an annualized basis of approximately $16 billion. Its success is even more impressive when one considers that this chain got its start in the mid-1950's. Further, the second largest chain, Burger King, is less than 40% the size of McDonald's. In many ways, McDonald's alone has provided the role model for the many franchisers attracted by the continuing increased consumer demand for hospitality-type products and services. A listing of the Top 10 franchised restaurant and hospitality systems is shown on the following page.

TOP 10
FRANCHISED RESTAURANT CHAINS

Chain	1988 Franchised U.S. Units
1. McDonald's	6,149
2. Dairy Queen	4,551
3. Burger King	4,454
4. Kentucky Fried Chicken	3,637
5. Domino's Pizza	3,225
6. Pizza Hut	2,937
7. Subway Sandwiches	2,828
8. Baskin-Robbins	2,449
9. Wendy's Old Fashioned Hamburgers	2,445
10. Hardee's	2,038

TOP 10
FRANCHISED LODGING CHAINS

Lodging	1988 Total U.S. Rooms
1. Holiday Corp.	267,724
2. Best Western	170,360
3. Ramada	122,602
4. Quality International	114,542
5. Marriott	99,682
6. Hilton Hotels	96,075
7. The Sheraton Corp.	92,075
8. Days Inn of America	84,832
9. Howard Johnson	52,271
10. Motel 6	48,842

The essence of business format franchising is what, in fact, makes it such a powerful idea. It is characterized by an ongoing business and professional relationship between franchiser and franchisee that goes beyond product, service, and/or trademark.

It instead provides the entrepreneurial franchisee with a complete business concept including marketing strategy, operating plans and manuals, definitive standards, quality control, and a continuing program of assistance and guidance.

While franchising, of course, has had its share of those that have abused the system, there is no question that when one looks at the hospitality industry today, there is probably no other feasible way that the need for dedicated and talented management/owners could have been achieved without the concept of franchising. The benefits that have accrued to the public by virtue of "chaining" would simply not have occurred had something like franchising not existed. The ability to assemble a large number of entrepreneurial oriented individuals in a business system that keeps them motivated, dedicated, and loyal to their franchiser's philosophy and concept is simply a very powerful concept.

Some current illustrations of how franchising allows entrepreneurs to grow is typified by the recent success of two relatively new chains that wanted to expand rapidly. During 1988 Subway Sandwiches and Salads opened more than 1,000 new stores, and Domino's opened an additional 500 stores. During the most recent two year period, this represented an addition of more than 1,850 stores for Subway and nearly 1,000 new stores for Domino's. Forgetting whether or not their success will be long-term, their ability to open the number of units they have would not have been possible if they were to have attempted it on a company store only basis.

In an era where "big business" seems to have so many advantages and even within the food industry where the megamergers continue to cause major upheaval in the food processing side of the business, I find it reassuring that even though McDonald's or a Burger King may, in fact, be large corporations, the presence of healthy entrepreneurship provides a check and balance on the franchiser that will keep the system responsive to both the customer and the franchisee.

One has to look no further than what took place in the Fall of 1988 when Grand Metropolitan wanted to acquire The Pillsbury Company. Pillsbury's management used virtually every technique and tactic known to corporate management to avoid the takeover, but, as reported in the press at the time, the lack of support of the Burger King franchisees for Burger King and Pillsbury management ultimately may have been the factor that led to Grand Met being successful in accomplishing the merger. Frequent stories in the general business press quoted individual franchisees who typify successful "small business persons," and it is their voices that were heard the loudest, not those of the attorneys or the other advisors who seem to play such a prominent role in these kinds of transactions.

In my judgment it is almost impossible to comtemplate what the hospitality industry would be like if the idea of franchisee and franchiser had not only been developed but had not been used for the ultimate benefit for all partners by the likes of McDonald's and others. By offering a vehicle to simultaneously reduce the risk of failure while providing the opportunity to "own the business," franchising is as close to a "win-win" as one can find in today's business environment.

New Challenges Require
Creative Solutions

Roger W. Coleman is President and Chief Executive Officer of Rykoff-Sexton, Inc., a foodservice manufacturer and distribution firm headquartered in Los Angeles, California. He is a diplomate of the Educational Foundation of the National Restaurant Association.

Question: What is the most creative idea you have ever experienced in the hospitality industry?

I have spent a good part of my life in the food distribution business, and in so doing I have spent a good many hours and have consumed a good many meals in foodservice establishments throughout the country. In addressing the subject of creativity, I want to turn the tables so to speak, to tell you what I see as an informed customer.

While the image of a chef artfully carving baby vegetables may well conjure illusions of highly creative talent, one doesn't have to be an artist to partake in the myriad of creative opportunities to be found within the foodservice industry.

Some may consider creativity in our industry an anathema, but recent innovations suggest quite the contrary. In fact, if one has a creative bent and enjoys the challenge of making the ordinary exciting, the foodservice industry holds a lot in store.

A look at the industry today demonstrates the role creative thinking plays on a day-to-day basis. Restaurateurs are discovering opportunities in the changing lifestyles of the general population. Burgeoning numbers of working couples, increasing health-consciousness, and a booming demand for carry-out foods have prompted creative responses.

An increase in two-career families is leading many people to spend less time in their kitchens, more time in restaurants. Some want to eat and run. Others enjoy lingering over a five-course meal.

Expanding consumer needs and preferences have resulted in a boost in the number and variety of restaurants, as well as a proliferation of drive-through and fast-food establishments.

As a result, foodservice professionals have developed such conveniences as improved plastic packaging, which allows restaurants to sell carry-out salads that maintain freshness; and separate cash and food windows, which speed up the drive-through process.

Innovative chefs are measuring success by response to their unusual dishes. They are blending ethnic flavors and ingredients, writing recipes that trim calories but retain their taste, complementing traditional dishes with light sauces and artistic presentations, and inventing no-guilt desserts.

Many diners view eating out not only as a convenience, but as an escape from the mundane — a chance to enjoy good food presented and served with extraordinary flair. Meeting the demands of sophisticated consumers attuned to popular foods, serving styles, and restaurant environments dictates that foodservice professionals be sensitive to emerging trends.

In recent years, foodservice professionals have scrambled to capture the business of health-conscious consumers, many of whom are reducing their intake of caffeine and saturated fat while increasing their consumption of fresh produce and high-fiber foods.

Most restaurants now serve brewed decaffeinated coffee. Because decaf drinkers worry that refills are caffeinated, many don't order coffee. The use of color-banded coffee pots to identify decaf — a creative idea that almost has become an industry standard — have since reassured customers they're getting what they ordered.

The popularity of healthful foods also has inspired creative chefs to re-examine their menus and cooking methods. Fried fish has succumbed to broiled, and plain baked potatoes have replaced potatoes au gratin. Breakfast repertoires have extended beyond bacon and eggs to include healthful whole grain pancakes and waffles, bran muffins, and oatmeal.

Creativity plays an obvious role in contract design. Because a coffee shop or a white table cloth restaurant is likely to attract different customers, restaurant operators study the markets they want to attract before determining their setting, menu, and pricing.

In addition to lending ambiance to dining rooms, contract designers are making kitchens efficient. That means assuring that food traffic flows smoothly through delivery, preparation, and presentation; maximizing profits through efficient use of time, products, and space;

and ensuring safety. These demands require versatile equipment in a well-organized space.

Contract designers plan kitchens to meet industry needs. As consumer demands have risen for light fare and fresh produce, designers have increased counter space for preparation and introduced walk-in refrigerators to replace oversized freezers.

Kitchens cramped by growing preparation areas have necessitated the use of compact, multi-purpose equipment. An example is the combioven which operates simultaneously as a convection oven, a range, and a steamer.

Energy conservation is another challenging problem for contract designers, who are slashing gas and electricity use with such innovations as low temperature dishwashers, "makeup air" exhaust hoods, and electronic equipment that dispenses chemicals reducing product waste due to inaccurate measurement. Low temperature dishwashers use tepid water and a special chemical in place of 180 degree water in the final rinse. While traditional exhaust hoods draw air from a restaurant interior and expel it outside, the make-up air exhaust hood draws and tempers from the outdoors as much as 80 percent of the air it uses.

Concerns for kitchen safety underscore the creative need to revise equipment safety features. Sharp bladed knives, for example, are usually camouflaged by their black handles. To ensure knives are visible to kitchen staffs, product designers have developed a bright handled cutlery set.

Clearly, both challenges and solutions in this rapidly changing industry span a broad spectrum. For foodservice professionals just launching their careers, accepting those challenges will mean keeping abreast of and forecasting change while constantly seeking creative solutions. The reward for creative thinking will be the ability to meet tomorrow's demands with answers that will reach consumers today.

Self-Esteem Is Essential
To Building A Team

Jim L. Peterson is President and Chief Executive Officer of Whataburger Inc., a regional quick service chain headquartered in Corpus Christi, Texas. He is past President of the National Restaurant Association.

Question: What key qualities and values do you look for in assessing management talent?

The most important characteristic of a potentially successful manager is high self-esteem. This must be developed and nurtured through a positive value system based primarily on the following qualities:

Honesty and integrity, empathy, industriousness, perserverance, the ability to enjoy life, concentration on key goals, and the ability to learn from both success and failure.

With this type of value system nurturing a high and confident self-esteem, one should then look for certain qualities which may already be in place. These qualities would have the potential to develop into management attributes.

The first such quality is the ability to plan each day, working toward solid objectives as they relate to business life, personal life, spiritual life, etc.

Next is to maintain a progressive attitude, so that each tomorrow will offer the challenge of doing things better than you did today, and the overriding necessary ability to pass this philosophy on and develop it within other people.

Then there is the need to listen; not only listen intently, but study the habits and the specifics of what people are saying, so you can get to know them better and respond to their needs.

In any case, you want to be sure that people can help develop and reinforce the high standards of your business.

Hopefully, you will have learned from past failures and will not become discouraged. You must allow others to try and to fail. Failure should be allowed in a growing, imaginative business.

Strong managers will have a sense of understanding about role models. They themselves will be models and will know how to identify others who can be used to form the foundation of how they want things done.

They should understand the necessity of constant performance measurement and frequent follow-ups related thereto. They should always be able to articulate how they will identify and recognize achievements that help the business grow and prosper.

In this instance, I'm not talking about the quality of being able to merely follow a structured plan incentive, but rather the quality and interest of a potential manager to reward others through frequent praise and constructive criticism when necessary.

Finally, and probably the most important, is the quality of being a team player and the ability to inspire team play and peer group cooperation among others.

There is no other business that requires such teamwork and comaraderie as does the hospitality industry. Without team spirit, a manager will constantly find himself working alone and pulling from all sides to get any sort of job done. With a team effort, with everyone helping each other, the job is so remarkably easy that few could imagine how it could be done any other way.

It should be clearly noted here that none of these important management qualities, as they relate to people, can be achieved without a high level of self-esteem. I have found that low self-esteem makes it impossible to inspire a team of any sort. The various qualities necessary to fully develop other employees cannot be attained without a high level of self-esteem to provide the base to make others actually feel better about what they are doing.

I have not discussed work habits, work patterns, administrative capabilities, bookwook, etc. These are important. However, my experience shows that if the above qualities and values are present, all else can either be learned or accomplished through other people on the team.

I hope these principles will be helpful, and that we can all gain a great deal as we continue to create new ways and means of being more effective leaders in a constantly changing world.

People will be thinking of new dimensions in the foodservice industry during the next five years. Labor costs will be replaced by human-resource accounting, and our types of businesses will be valued just as much in terms of people assets as in financial assets.

For those who recognize this, tremendous opportunities lie ahead. Those who truly understand that the new balance sheet will reflect people and their skills as a true asset of the business will indeed emerge as the successful leaders of tomorrow.

When You Are Green You Grow

James D. Cockman is former Chairman and Chief Executive Officer of PYA/Monarch Inc., foodservice distributors, headquartered in Greenville, South Carolina and is currently Chairman of Sara Lee Foodservice. He is also Vice Chairman of the Board of Directors of the International Foodservice Distributors Association (IFDA).

Question: What is the best advice you ever received, and why do you regard it as such?

I believe leadership is the single most important ingredient as we look to the future. I am concerned that the message many of our people are receiving today is that business and government leaders alike are failing to fulfill their responsibilities in leadership and integrity. Therefore, I consider the question, "What is the best advice you ever received and why do you regard it as such?" difficult to respond to without considering integrity.

Frankly, I have given a great deal of thought to this and as a result have pondered many experiences and memories of the past. I came to the conclusion that the very best advice I ever received on leadership came from my father. He was not a formally educated individual but did have considerable people skills and was one of the best sales leaders I have ever known.

I was raised on a small farm in eastern North Carolina with four brothers and one sister. All of us had to work in order to supplement the family income. One of the crops we raised was tomatoes. My father always made it a key point to teach us the art of selecting and packing tomatoes.

On one occasion it became evident that my father was more interested in giving me some leadership advice than in just picking tomatoes.

71

He picked a large, ruby red ripe tomato and a green tomato. When I inquired why he picked the green one after having spent so much time teaching us the precise state of ripeness, he said that in addition to picking tomatoes for the market he wanted to give me key points to consider as I thought about a career.

He said when you are ripe you rot, but when you are green you grow. He said you should live your life with the quest for increased knowledge that will result in continual growth. He said the only thing that any individual truly owns in this world is his or her reputation and that this will live longer than you will. Therefore, it is important not to misrepresent your tomatoes by putting the ripe on top and the green ones on the bottom. In other words, always deliver on the goods and do what you say you are going to do when you say you are going to do it.

I was 35 years old before the full significance of that afternoon really hit me. I was in my office in Manhattan struggling with a particular business problem that had the potential of offering extraordinary growth as well as impacting my personal and business reputation. I am quite confident that if I had not had that experience in the tomato field I might never have selected the path that would both enhance my growth and reputation. The long and short of it is that people will not continue to follow leaders who are dishonest. Individuals do have a choice as to what kind of reputation they would prefer, and reputations do live longer than people.

I selected this as some of the best advice I have ever received because it has prompted me to look at each situation from the other individual's perspective and to treat customers and employees as I would like to be treated. This principle has worked for us and for our company.

Get Ahead By Proving You Deserve What You Already Have

Roberto C. Goizueta is Chairman of the Board and Chief Executive Officer of Atlanta based The Coca-Cola Company, a position he has held since 1981. He has served The Coca-Cola Company for over 35 years.

Question: What is the best advice you ever received, and why do you regard it as such?

Leadership is not an academic discipline that can be learned in a classroom or a book. There are, of course, people we all know who are "born leaders," but for most of us, leadership skills are acquired through the application of sage advice and "on the job" experience. As I look back over my career with The Coca-Cola Company, I realize how much I have benefited from timely advice given to me by a wide spectrum of people from all over the world.

As you can imagine, after 35 years with one company I have received lots of advice — sometimes more than I felt necessary. A couple of thoughts, however, summarize a common thread running through most of the advice I have received. The first thought is quite straightforward; work hard on the job at hand and someone sooner or later will notice the results of your work and then notice you.

In a society where people increasingly expect — and sometimes demand — instant recognition, this advice is often difficult to follow. We tend to look beyond the task before us and anticipate the challenges that lie ahead. Maybe we feel that a job we are asked to do is insignificant or beneath our capabilities, but the best way to gain additional responsbility is to prove you deserve what you already have.

Robert W. Woodruff, the late patriarch of The Coca-Cola Company, made a related thought his credo: "There is no limit to what a man can do or where he can go if he doesn't mind who gets the credit." In fact, your objective should be to reflect credit on your colleagues, your supervisors, and your organization. Strive to make your ideas so good that your superiors want to make them their own.

A second bit of advice that has served me well for many years is to keep a sense of humor. As a bit of doggerel reminds us, "It's easy enough to be pleasant when life goes along like a song, but the man worthwhile is the man who can smile when everything goes dead wrong." How easy it is to let the anxieties and problems of the world drag us down and snuff out our sense of humor! One secret to dealing successfully with our inevitable failures is to put them behind us as quickly as possible, and I have always found humor a great help in speeding the process along.

Keeping a sense of humor is also important to maintaining others' morale. I am reminded of the old World War II movie where a unit is surrounded and under heavy fire and the platoon leader quips, "O.K., boys, now we've got 'em where we want 'em." A little humor can go a long way toward helping people overcome seemingly impossible obstacles.

Work wholeheartedly at the task at hand and inject a little humor when things look their worst. This is advice I have received in one form or another since I was a young boy. It has stood me in good stead both personally and professionally.

Why is this the best advice I ever received? First, it has worked for me. Second, at the risk of circular logic, I find myself passing it along to others as others passed it along to me. Is there any better criterion for advice than that it has passed the test of time?

Incentives Yield Productivity

Leon W. (Pete) Harman is President and Chief Executive Officer of Harman Management Corporation headquartered in Los Altos, California. The company operates over 235 Kentucky Fried Chicken stores. He is an honorary director of the National Restaurant Association.

Question: What is the best advice you ever received, and why do you regard it as such?

The best advice I ever received was in 1951 from an instructor who taught a short course sponsored by NRA at the University of Chicago. By attending this course, I also had the pleasure of meeting Colonel Sanders, who was a student as well.

The instructor proceeded to provide information about a study done at General Motors. Every level of employee at General Motors, even their top leadership, was involved in this study which measured one's productive capacity. The research revealed that General Motors had one of the best pre-study productivity rates among major industrial companies in the nation, 46 percent!

The instructor, I realized, emphasized the fact that if production levels were raised above the 46 percent level, think of the possibilities: you could surpass the competition; run more efficiently; and raise employee moral, just to name a few of the many benefits.

I had not realized until that time how inefficient the labor force was, and it made me believe that I could do something about it.

In 1951, my wife, Arline, and I had a 100 seat restaurant in Salt Lake City, Utah, where we introduced Kentucky Fried Chicken to the world with Colonel Sanders' first franchise agreement. (Harlan Sanders and I had gotten to know one another at that seminar, and I first learned about his chicken product with its special blend of herbs and spices.) I realized then that I could increase production by implementing some simple philosophies.

I wanted to create a positive, happy environment where people liked to come to work.

As our restaurants expanded and our number of employees increased, we initiated cash incentives tied to the profitability of the unit for store managers.

In 1958, when we opened a fourth store 40 miles away in Ogden, Utah, which we couldn't visit every day, I decided to sell 40 percent of the stock in that store to the managers who were willing to go beyond the normal productivity limits. They made it work, and up to this day it is still working! By taking this one step further, I rewarded achievements beyond the normal capacity at all levels of our workforce with such things as service pins, plaques, etc.

Today, with over 4,000 employees stretched across four states and over 235 Kentucky Fried Chicken restaurants, I have found that this system has made us a productive company. Along with the store stock ownership, other forms of recognition have expanded over the years to include one week paid incentive trips to resort destinations such as Hawaii; a corporate name established for our KFC restaurant after the employees who have made significant contributions to Harman's; several different programs involving custom made lapel pins; and our annual black-tie awards banquet where our top managers win a two week trip of their choice anywhere in the world.

I feel it is very important to develop people from within. With this system, employees learn all phases of the job and can look forward to upward movement.

You also need to measure success and growth of employees along the way. Companies will only be as successful as their employees are committed, and it is possible to improve productivity if you take good care of your employees.

Our growth has been rapid and successful from our first small restaurant to over 235 restaurants throughout the western United States. And, we're not done yet!

Get Tough, Ladies

Louise O'Sullivan is President of Groen/A Dover Industries Company headquartered in Elk Grove, Illinois. She is a 1989 recipient of the Market Mover Award presented by the Marketing Agents for the Food Service Industry.

Question: What is the best advice you ever received, and why do you regard it as such?

The best advice I ever received was a simple two-word phrase that at the time, significantly impacted my lifestyle and eventually altered my personality. At the risk of sounding like a wimp who has had sand kicked in her face, the two word phrase that had such impact was "Get Tough."

Little girls grow up being taught to please others. Little boys grow up being taught to best others. Unless you get special direction as a little girl, your immediate goals often revolve around being liked, being accepted, and (will my Mother's words ever stop ringing in my ear?) "BEING NICE."

Much of pleasing others and being accepted means meeting expectations. My parents' expectations were simple: "As long as you *do your best* in everything, it's good enough for us." What a burden! Mom pushed it a little further. Midst her echoes of "be nice," she had a unique way of encouraging us to do better. Upon triumphantly bringing home a score of 95% on a test, Mom would smile and respond, "That's nice, honey. Um, did anyone get a higher grade?" She knew how to be tough.

With a double major in psychology and education, and a Master's Degree in child guidance (which I use more in business than I ever did in teaching), my early modus operandi was to do whatever it took to get the job done while still being liked and appreciated.

In the meantime, my male counterparts were out blocking and tackling, marching and fighting, and, most importantly, surviving in a very tough world. While I was winning suburban Teacher of the Year Awards and attempting to raise our children to be independent and responsible, the males of my generation were returning (or not) from Vietnam, playing softball and football and golf on weekends, and climbing the corporate ladders. Getting tough came as a natural experience to them.

When an opportunity came to enter the business world after four years of teaching primary school and four years of substitute teaching (I took everything no one else wanted — boy's gym, music, etc.) combined with raising babies, doing homebound tutoring, and establishing a parents' co-op preschool, I jumped at it. Groen needed a writer for advertising and PR; I needed a new challenge with more pay.

For two years I was on Groen's payroll as an advertising consultant, travelling, working with end-users and reps two to four days a week while keeping my fingers in the teaching pie as well.

Suddenly it was career decision time. Both my children were now school-age and my "dream job," that of a kindergarten teacher, was offered. Looking for statement about potential, I went to Lew Burns, then our V.P. Sales/Marketing, to ask about my future at Groen.

He listened carefully to my presentation of how much I had enjoyed the past two years, yet how incredibly aware I was of how much I *didn't know*. He was patient as I explained that while business was really exciting, all my education had been to be an educator, and that my highest turn on to date was to inspire and excite a child's mind. If I was going to stay, it was clear that I would have to get some business education, probably, and an MBA from a school with a program for non-business majors. He waited while I came to the obvious closing question, "If I stay at Groen, what's in it for me?"

Lew responded with four short words; "You can be president." Wow, did he have my number! Then he expanded. "First of all," he said, "we think you've demonstrated that nothing stands in your way when you ᵥant to achieve something — so, if you are going to invest the time in a business education, do it right. We'll send you to the University of Chicago's Executive Program. Secondly, to reach the presidency of this company you've got to do two things in this industry. One is *Get Visible* — get involved, be outstanding; and the other is *Get Tough* — stop worrying about who likes you, and start earning their respect. Learn to negotiate win-win. Set your goals high and dream big. Envision yourself in the President's chair. Now mentally put your feet up on the desk, see yourself there, and it will happen for you.

Amazingly, I had used that mental imaging strategy for years. I believe your mind controls your body, and you can cure yourself of disease. I believe a stadium full of totally concentrating fans can move a football down a field toward the goal post. I believe that people who are positive and excited about life have less illness. Lew suggested that a book he was very high on, Joseph Murphy's *The Power of Your Subconscious Mind* (Bantam, 1963), be added to my library. It was terrific, illustrating amazing stories of people who practiced mental imaging and were thusly rewarded.

That was 1978. Lew told me in his own way that this company cared about me and, also, it went first class. In 1980, I got that MBA degree while competing with the sharpest bunch of "killers" I had ever come across. The XP-44 University of Chicago class of 56 men and six women was a coterie of winners, all leaders, all hand-picked by their companies to be future presidents and general managers. Boy, did I work hard to get tough fast — this was baptism by fire! We worked at our jobs all week, went to class on alternate Fridays and Saturdays, and had evening study groups once or twice weekly for two years. I learned as much from my peers as I did in the classroom. And, in 1985 I became President of Groen.

But those two words "get tough," to someone who was the May Queen in 8th grade, were alien advice. "Get visible" I could do; the equipment industry was run by men. With luck, my uniqueness alone guaranteed visibility, but toughness, ugh! That was not what nice girls worked for.

Nevertheless, since that's what it took, I was determined to work on it, and it turned out to be the best advice I ever received.

It required calling on all the coaching experience I'd ever had, to lead people without bossing them. It called on enthusiasm and good will, always coupled with accountability and results orientation. Inspirationally, it mandated a competitiveness and winning attitude that would rival any Vince Lombardi protegé. In short, toughness meant setting high standards and watching people surpass them. It meant firing a friend because the benefit of the many doubts had finally run out, and he would be happier elsewhere. It meant sharpening risk assessment skills to a fine point, then employing them in every strategic analysis. It meant becoming an expert in your specific area, so that those who never expected much from a woman in a technical field were amazed and subsequently loyal friends.

Getting tough has great range. Getting tough allowed me to have the courage to zing back a one liner when a customer made an indelicate remark which embarrassed the group instead of just smiling and praying to drop invisibly through the floor. Getting tough encouraged me to ask the point blank question when interviewing a job candidate, "How do you expect working for a woman might affect your performance?" Getting tough mandated asking subordinates questions they could shine at answering until you come to one they couldn't, so they'd continually leave challenged.

My husband, Bob Oslin, who is a genius *and* a "killer," had lunch recently with a long time pal of mine (from first grade). This talented lady raised a family of three, then returned to law school, and is now a practicing attorney in a major downtown Chicago law firm. Somehow they got to discussing what makes women successful leaders, and Bob launched into a discussion of how I attribute much of my success to "being tough." Mary Ellen said, "Louise, the one who used to cry if someone looked at her cross-eyed?" Bob smiled, "That's the one!"

"Get tough" to a curly haired girl with strong drive for recognition meant more than the Marine image of mental and physical toughness. Lew Burns' "get tough" meant recognizing and calling upon inner talent that might not be utilized by someone striving to "be nice," then using your niceness to make it a win-win situation. Sincerity and genuine caring are part of a tough personality when one's priorities are correct.

A leader must possess the inner strength that makes self-satisfaction and pride in others equally rewarding. Inner toughness showed me how to conquer the urge to examine events on a personal basis and, instead, to strive harder for success of the team.

"Get tough" meant understanding that a good woman executive is never one of the boys nor should she want to be. No matter what, she's different. If she uses that difference to the ultimate advantage, she combines the tough side with the gentle side, the way few men can.

Lew Burns' "Get tough" meant: Make all the "killers" aware of your nature, then catch them off guard with your niceness. It works!

It Makes A Difference Who Is Boss

Robert H. Power is a partner in Nut Tree, a diversified restaurant, bakery, candy, merchandise, and toy complex located in Nut Tree, California, which is approximately halfway between San Francisco and Sacramento. He is past President of the National Restaurant Association.

Question: What is the best advice you ever received, and why do you regard it as such?

The best advice I ever received was through the assimilation of an experience as a private, 90th Infantry Division, in the Battle of Bastogne and the Battle of the Rhineland under the command of General George C. Patton.

The lesson was very simple and direct, "It makes a difference who is boss." From the first day I entered the 358th Infantry Regiment 90th Division as a replacement private, I felt the "command" charge which emitted from Patton's officers (management).

The Captain welcomed us with a cleaned up version of the opening speech in *Patton* (the movie), "Tomorrow, men, when you engage the enemy, you will double time towards them . . . You hear! You will double time towards them!"

The next day we were ordered to abandon our overcoats as a chilling wind blew over the snow covered Ardens. "Can't run in them," the Captain explained. Spirits were high because it was accepted by all that Patton knew how to win, which was the only reason we believed there was a future for any of us, but Berlin seemed a long way away.

As we started down the slopes of the Rhineland breaking the Siegfried Line, I heard a hoop and a holler from behind, "Handy Ho Komsey Here," and we all joined in that "double time" maneuver that fleeced the woods of the enemy with little loss of life — that day.

I only survived three weeks of this experience, but when I returned to California and someone asked, "What was it like?" I merely said, "I learned it makes a difference who's boss."

I never met General Patton who influenced my management concepts the most. However, I now know men who personally knew him and they have refused to this day to view *Patton* (the movie) for fear it will influence their real image of Patton, the man.

I asked a former Judge Advocate Corps officer about his favorite Patton story; everyone who ever knew Patton had stories about how he inspired and won the hearts of his men.

This now Superior Court Judge quietly related, "It was on the Mosell and the order came from above to our Colonel that tomorrow at dawn the 358th Infantry shall cross the river." The Colonel who received the order was disheartened because his troops were in houses on the west side of the Mosell, the Germans were on the east side, and the river had steep banks and ran swift. It appeared to be a suicidal mission. At that point, General Patton paid a rare visit to the regiment and the Colonel asked, "General, tomorrow we are going to cross the river at dawn. Could you give me the best advice on how you would do this?" Patton, swaggering, with his ivory handled revolvers charged up three flights of stairs, down a long hallway, threw open the windows, and looked up and down the Mosell with the German gun emplacements on the roof tops on the other side. As he strode down the hall he said, "Colonel, you will cross the river as ordered!" The Colonel gave a stunned, "Yes, sir!" However, as General Patton mounted his jeep, he shot back over his shoulder, "Colonel, but the time and place I will tell you later."

The 358th and 90th Division a few weeks later moved north from the Mosell to Bastogne in one of the historic marches in the annals of war. Because of General Patton's personal intervention, they lived to indoctrinate me into what became the philosophy of a lifetime, "It matters who is boss."

I think this is exactly why some restaurants prosper and others wither. One owner or manager leads, inspires, and directs with wisdom, giving proper times and places to do the task expected; and most of all, he or she gives it a personal hand and caring attention.

Establish Interaction, Not Insulation

Rosemary S. Garbett is President and sole owner of Los Tios Mexican Restaurants, Inc., a ten-unit chain headquartered in Houston, Texas. She is past President of the Houston Restaurant Association and has served on the Board of Directors of the Texas Restaurant Association.

Question: In general terms, what was your most vexing management problem, and how did you manage your way through it?

There comes a time in the life of every business when the owner is faced with a universal truth; One person cannot do it all. As the owner and President of a multi-unit restaurant business, I wanted to expand and try new things; and, therefore, I wanted to reorganize to provide more time to delve into the areas of expansion, growth and innovation.

An entrepreneur builds a business from the beginning never fully understanding how big it is going to get. Then one day the business becomes big and successful, but it still needs innovation and close supervision. I arrived at that point and thought if I had specialists in a few key positions with a professional education and knowledge, they would be able to dispatch many details quicker than I could, especially since I have only a high school education and was a housewife when I took over the business. I thought that if I had an operations manager with a degree and some years of actual experience, that person would be qualified by education and training to get right to the heart of problems and solve them quickly. An operations manager with a degree would have to be better than I am and would work smarter, I rationalized. I also thought that if I had a controller who was a CPA, that person could handle the financial details of the business better than I could. These people would be great, and because of those special skills they would know already how to do what I had been learning on the job.

Does this sound familiar to you? Those without a degree often feel others with a degree know how to do things better and quicker. Attempting to come to terms with this was and may still be my most vexing management problem, one that requires all of my skills and leadership to manage.

I first went into the open market to hire an operations manager. When I say "open market," I didn't use a recruiter because I thought I knew what I was looking for in terms of education, background, and experience.

The want ads in the newspaper produced several good candidates. One was uniquely qualified by education. He had that coveted degree and he also had experience. Not experience in a multi-unit operation such as Los Tios, but experience in a larger corporation which I then believed was better.

The operations manager would have these responsibilities. He would be the link between me and my units. He would see to it that the unit managers were there when each unit opened and when it closed. He would communicate our principles of quality and customer satisfaction to each manager and see to it that they communicated it to their employees.

The operations manager would be responsible for all Los Tios res-taurants, accountable only to me. Everyone in the units would report to the operations manager, either directly or indirectly.

I hired my Director of Operations and put him to work.

I now realize I was coveting insulation. I wanted to be insulated from the day to day. I was delighted with my accomplishment. I was heading toward that dreamed of time when I would be able to lean back and think seriously of IDEAS. Really think of IDEAS without the pressure of the day to day.

I then turned my attention to identifying a controller. The controller would handle all of the financial segments of Los Tios restaurants, i.e., the daily receipts, the inventory, the bank deposits, the quarterly reports, etc. Everything financial except the yearly tax return and my personal finances would be handled by the controller. I found a person so perfectly qualified and highly recommended, that he was hired quickly. He had a Masters Degree and was a CPA as well with a good background in a large accounting firm.

Let's go back a little.

I was performing all of these tasks myself before I got my idea for creating these two positions. When a business is small and struggling as mine was, you perform these tasks not by training but by instinct. They must be done and who better to do them than the owner. Besides, in the beginning money was so tight that the more I did for myself the more chance the business had to survive.

An independently owned business takes on the character and values of the owner. It is an extension of everything the owner believes.

Enter now a new influence: An operations manager who wants to do it his way. Wants to hire his own people. Wants the menu to reflect his thinking. Wants his stamp on everything.

One might think it was a clear clash of personalities. Not really. It was a clash of cultures. The first person I hired did not work by the same clock I did. He frequently had long lunches outside the business with suppliers and others. When I required daily staffing sheets on my desk by a certain time, they wouldn't be there. I also realized something else. My operations manager had come from a large corporation where he had people above and below him to insulate him from his day to day. He had in his previous position what I was trying to achieve by hiring him. He began building those levels of insulation for himself. So the company began needing extra people who insulated the operations manager from me and from his subordinates.

I learned that I had another vexing problem.

I discovered I was not only insulated, but that I was unaware that the character and values of the business I built were changing. Frankly, I had lost direct touch and I didn't like it. By creating one level of insulation for myself, I inadvertantly created other levels of insulation. That would never do.

After a year and a half the operations manager left by mutual agreement. I assumed day to day operations management again, but I still held on to my idea.

I went to an outside recruiter and told him of my need. He assured me he could solve my problem.

In a short time he had identified a number of qualified applicants. He screened them and sent over the ones who fit the job description and qualifications. I hired a second operations manager. The same thing happened. It took two years, but history repeated itself. I again took over day-to-day operations responsibility.

I have been told that those who build businesses have eyes that see special things and ears that hear special things.

In case you are wondering about the controller position, that path was different because of the nature of the position, but the outcome was the same. The first controller stayed two years. The second one stayed a year and a half.

A business is built by doing what needs to be done.

There is a level of innovation and market penetration a successful business operator achieves that permits the business to grow and prosper.

After three years of trying, I discoverd I simply couldn't insulate myself from the business no matter how large it grew.

After three years of trying, I learned that the special on-the-job skills I had acquired to grow the business were indeed "special." No amount of formal education in the mind of another would provide a short cut to the same end.

I gathered all of the details I had tried to give to the two new positions. I then delegated small bits of each position to my trusted people without overloading them.

I preserved the character and values of the business I had built.

I now know I can grow and continue to prosper. I know that I must keep my eyes and ears open and never lose sight of what made this business what it is. My ability to do what needs to be done when it needs to be done for the good of the customer is foremost in my mind.

Customers line up at your door day after day for a reason. They know there is something special on the other side. That something special is a reflection of you.

Test For The Best

Jack C. Maier is Chairman and President of Frisch's Restaurant Inc. headquartered in Cincinnati, Ohio. He is an Honorary Director of the National Restaurant Association.

Question: In general terms, what was your most vexing management problem, and how did you manage your way through it?

Frisch's most vexing management problem occurred as we were growing and involved in the selection of store managers. Incorporated in 1947, by 1958 we had about 25 company owned and operated restaurants and franchisees with whom we worked closely. At the time our management selection process was one that gave us a different caliber of manager depending on who was doing the interviewing. A good interviewer having an off day could be disastrous for the selection process, and there was no consistency from one interviewer to another.

Our thought at the time was to discuss this with Industrial Psychologists, to see if there was a testing procedure that would recognize the aptitude and attitude conducive to restaurant management. To begin with, there were not very many Industrial Pscyhologists then in the marketplace. We found a couple to talk to, but they informed us that the only testing background that was available was for job applicants for bank tellers or salespeople, but not for management at any level. No retailer had taken any interest in any other form of industrial testing.

We proceeded with these folks in an attempt to determine the characteristics of a good manager. We spent a lot of time and effort testing our existing management team, sorting them into "good," "bad," and "poor." We had the advantage of using the actual results of their performance, plus our intuition. We knew how they controlled their costs, the quality of employees each had hired, and how they supervised. But, using a written test to match a manager's effectiveness against personal characteristics was a revolutionary idea for any industry.

What resulted was the nucleus of a testing program that we felt could identify a consistently performing individual. Hindsight reveals that we were successful, because our top Operations Management went through the testing program and were consistently promoted from within.

That's not to say the testing procedures have remained the same, because thirty years later we're still putting a lot of time and effort into refining this program to meet today's needs. We need to be sure that candidates have the talent, personality, and innate skills that are required to be a professional manager in foodservice. With those abilities to work with, the training programs then have an opportunity to stretch our people, giving them the chance to grow both personally and professionally.

Let me emphasize the word stretch. We want them to want to reach out for the objectives that are before them, we don't stretch them unrealistically however, so that they tear.

Today's tests deliver managers that provide the consistency and control functions allowing the company to deliver to the consumer a stable, consistent product.

We've learned to be innovative over time. People in management today are different than thirty years ago, reflecting the change in age or gender of the candidates as well as the needs of employees and consumers. Governmental regulations and compliance alone put an unusual burden on new people. Perceptive testing helps Frisch's to identify the individual most likely to succeed as a professional manager in our restaurants.

Moving Out Of A Comfort Zone

Warren Quinley is Managing Partner of Pannell Kerr Forster, the international firm of certified public accountants and consultants. He is based in Atlanta, Georgia.

Question: In general terms, what was your most vexing management problem, and how did you manage your way through it?

In the early 1980's, I headed the consulting division of Pannell Kerr Forster's Atlanta office. At that time, a significant portion of our consulting practice was conducting feasibility studies, financial analyses, and similar services designed to assist restaurants, hotels, and other real estate clients in securing financing for viable projects.

It was about this time that interest rates skyrocketed and new development came to a standstill.

Through our firm's professional education programs and a lot of personal on-the-job training, we had developed an excellent staff of consultants and now they had no work. I knew it would take years to rebuild such a talented team. Furthermore, these people had been loyal to PKF, and we felt obligated to them. On the other hand, good business judgment dictated that we could not pay them to sit idly in the office day after day. Would we have to let the entire department go?

It's easy to manage when things are going great, when customers are lined up for your goods or services. It's quite another thing when you know there is just no demand out there for your service. But, that's when management earns its pay.

One of the first things I did was to analyze the cause of the business decline and to determine whether it was likely to be a short- or long-term problem. The answer would dictate the action that had to be taken. In this case, it became obvious that the downturn would last many months, perhaps a year or two. I knew that we couldn't simply ride the storm out. Not only would such an alternative prove costly for the firm, but our personnel would not grow professionally during this period of time.

The next thing we did was sit down with the employees involved and level with them about the situation and the results of our analysis. They are bright people who understood what was going on in the economy and could see how it was adversely affecting the demand for the particular types of consulting services they provided.

Working through this situation then became a task for both management and employees. The firm made certain commitments to the employees, and, in turn, the employees agreed to take some time off to travel abroad or do other things their busy schedules had not and would not later permit. It was important that we stayed close to the employees during this stressful time. My door was always open to them, and we frequently met at scheduled intervals.

More significantly, however, this situation caused me to challenge these employees to break out of their respective comfort zones, their specific areas of expertise and investigate several related areas of service badly needed by the hospitality industry. These people became much more versatile and, as a result, valuable to the firm and its clients. In the process, the firm developed several new lines of business, and I learned a valuable lesson about having too many eggs in a single basket. From that point on, the consultants in my department were cross-trained, and we marketed what we now term "integrated services" which addresses a much broader range of client needs. It was a difficult time, but I believe we weathered it well, and benefited from it in the long term.

Growing Up Fast

Ella Brennan is a member of the famous Brennan family of New Orleans, Louisiana. She is co-owner of Commander's Place and Mr. B's, both located in New Orleans; and Brennans of Houston, located in that Texas metropolis. She is the recipient of numerous awards since she started in the restaurant business at the age of 17.

Question: In general terms, what was the most agonizing decision you ever made, and how did it affect you professionally and personally?

There are two things which came to mind immediately as I considered my reply to this question. The first was the recollection of the day my oldest brother, Owen, died. The New Orleans newspaper ran a banner headline of enormous size that read, "Owen Brennan Dead at 45." The impression of those words will be with me for as long as I live. We were in the process of moving to a new location as our lease on the old location was up, and we had leased the new location and had to open in six months. My role up to this time had been all operations oriented and now came an unbelievable financial responsibility.

The new restaurant *had* to be a success — *had to be!* So, I learned what work was all about. I delayed marriage for one and a half years, and with all my family pitching in together we got the new restaurant open.

I am pleased to say it was a success from day one, but what lessons had to be learned.

Professionally, I learned common sense and logical thinking will take you a long way. Personally, I learned the true meaning of family and friends.

A second event also occurs to me when used in the context of an "agonizing decision." When I was very young I had to terminate a long time employee who was not capable of performing at a higher level. The employee had taught me a lot, but we were growing and he was not. He was a good man and a loyal employee, and here I was, a kid, firing him. This type of situation causes you to grow up fast. Professionally, I learned that when hard decisions need to be made it's best to approach them directly and with immediacy. Delay doesn't help anybody or anything. Personally, I learned that some of the toughest decisions in life are "people decisions," but you still need to act on them.

An LBO — Staying The Course

J. Douglas Johnson is Co-Chairman, President, and Chief Executive Officer of G.S. Blodgett Corporation, a foodservice equipment manufacturer headquartered in Burlington, Vermont. He is a member of the Board of Directors of the National Association of Food Equipment Manufacturers (NAFEM).

Question: In general terms, what was the most agonizing decision you ever made, and how did it affect you professionally and personally?

Tough, hard business decisions are the easy ones. Whether to close a plant, invest heavily in a new product, or say no to a valued customer are choices generally dictated by circumstance.

But, what about decisions were several distinct courses of action are possible, each with dramatically different results?

These tend to be the truly agonizing decisions as I learned first hand when I decided to push all of my personal and business "chips" to the center of the table, stand up in a regularly scheduled board meeting and announce that I intended to buy G.S. Blodgett Company, a leading foodservice equipment manufacturer, in a leveraged buyout.

To many on the board, the very idea was sacrilege. After all, I was attempting to buy a 140-year-old closely-held company from a group of shareholders whose families have controlled the direction of Blodgett since the turn of the century. Furthermore, these shareholders had shown no inclination to sell.

In those few moments, I gambled my confortable position as President of one of the most successful and well respected companies in the industry for an uncertain future. And suddenly the financial resources, which I had so carefully accumulated to ensure my family's security, were no longer so secure. Those funds were in the stack of chips at the center of the table.

Time seemed to stand still as my words registered around the room.

How had I gotten to this point? What had I done?

In 1985, after spending years in the foodservice equipment business, first at Precision Industries in Miami and then in various subsidiaries of Alco Standard Corp. in Valley Forge, Pennsylvania, I was offered the position as president of Burlington, Vermont-based G.S. Blodgett Company. The job at the time seemed to offer unlimited opportunity and was particularly interesting because Blodgett, still privately held, had no family member to succeed its current President (soon to be Chairman).

I resigned my position, sold our house, and with a great deal of enthusiasm moved my family to Burlington. Blodgett, after all, was the world's leading manufacturer of ovens, and it wanted to become much more.

Blodgett had begun an expansion program in 1981 by acquiring the distinguished company of J.C. Pitman and Sons (now Pitco Frialator, Inc.), a leading manufacturer of deep fat frying equipment, founded in 1918; and Pitco Mastermatic, a manufacturer of conveyorized frying equipment for the food processing industry, founded in 1934. One year later it acquired Mastermatic, a manufacturer of conveyorized convection ovens.

Although Blodgett was expanding, little attempt was being made to properly structure its acquisitions. They were still operating as small independent companies, and as such were not reaping the benefits of being part of a larger organization.

My job was to continue Blodgett's expansion program, strengthen the individual companies, and fit them into a cohesive corporate structure.

The next two years shot by. Companies were reorganized, new top level managers were hired, and substantial investments were made in equipment, plants, and in acquiring the best technology available; Blodgett's expansion program also continued.

In the very first year, in fact, we were able to create a whole new category in foodservice equipment by introducing the then revolutionary Rational Combi-Oven/Steamer to the U.S. market. We also purchased Magikitch'n, a leading manufacturer of high quality broilers and griddles. Another company was added the following year.

Not everything went according to plan; we made our mistakes. In 1986, for example, with great fanfare Pitco Frialator introduced the

Turbo-Fry, utilizing revolutionary technology purchased from a small company in Georgia. Unfortunately, what we touted as the "biggest improvement in gas deep fat fryers to be introduced in 50 years" developed many unforeseen flaws and temporarily had to be withdrawn from the market.

Still, we were aggressively working toward our objectives, taking risks, and, most important of all, prospering. By the end of 1986, a new dynamic corporate structure was in place and The Blodgett Group was formally set up to manage all existing Blodgett Companies and future acquisitions.

But things were beginning to sour in the executive suite.

Blodgett was an old-line company whose management was conservative, and in the New England tradition, reticent. Even the idea of aggressive advertising and promotion was viewed with some disdain.

Furthermore, top executives, who had been with the company for years, were strongly resisting the many changes taking place. Adding to this was resentment in some cases of the new group of executives being brought in to run various operations which had functioned in the past with a minimal amount of supervision.

Eventually two camps developed, those who wanted to preserve the status quo and do things the way they had always been done and those who were eager to embrace new management techniques and opportunities to expand and become more competitive. The situation was particularly sensitive as the chairman and most of the board were allied with the first group.

I found myself in the unenviable position of trying to lead the forces for change while appeasing the advocates of the status quo. We entered a period of top management gridlock from which we would not emerge for almost three years.

Debates about direction raged, and a difficult situation was intensified when the chairman and his supporters began to usurp responsibility for the day-to-day operation of the company.

It was clear Blodgett had expanded as far as it could under the confines of its old corporate culture, and something had to be done.

Three courses of action presented themselves.

I could stay with the company, knuckle under, and continue in a job that had been transformed into something very different from the position for which I had been hired.

I could leave the company and everything I had accomplished there and move to another firm.

Or, I could buy the company from its current owners.

That idea, which at first I rejected as impossible, when reconsidered, made more and more sense.

The only stockholder and family member to be actively involved in Blodgett and who represented the interests of the other stockholders in the day-to-day running of the company, was the Chairman, but he was approaching retirement. When that happened it appeared likely Blodgett would be sold. Did it make sense, then, for me to abandon a company that I had helped to restructure and whose new top management was loyal to me?

The opportunity of a lifetime seemed to be within reach; this was my chance to grab the brass ring and make a difference. I would make a bid to buy the company and show the industry that such a move could be positive for everyone involved.

No decision can be made in a vacuum, however, and other factors had to be considered. Where would the financing come from? What would be the repercussions for the company, our employees, and our customers? And what would be the ultimate impact on my family, if I gambled everything and lost?

We were still living in a leased home and my wife and children were not yet feeling comfortable in New England. In addition, we had just gone to a great deal of trouble to have a beautiful piece of land rezoned so that we could build a house that we had carefully planned and designed. Construction, in fact, had just begun.

As I awaited the board's response, all of this flashed through my mind, but I knew I had made the right decision.

Little did I know that announcing my intention to buy Blodgett was to be merely the first small step in a three year odyssey that would test my mettle as a leader, personally and professionally. My odyssey would include a crash course in pulling together and executing leveraged buy-outs. It would include running a company while at the same time traveling almost constantly along with my new partner and friend, investment banker Samuel A. Hartwell, to raise money for the venture. And, ultimately, it would include my taking a forced leave of absence from Blodgett. Obviously, I would come to repeatedly question the wisdom of my decision as events moved forward.

Although the board was cool to my proposal, it agreed to consider it. Negotiations, however, were to drag on for months, as one offer after another was rejected with no counter proposals. But, rejection only strengthened my resolve.

Part of the problem, I was convinced, was that the chairman wasn't sure he really wanted to retire yet, and the board wasn't convinced that the best thing to do was to sell.

These were obstacles that I was sure could be overcome — until the board appointed Goldman Sachs to determine the Company's value in preparation to its being auctioned off.

Until then, the fact that Blodgett might be for sale was a closely guarded secret. Now, everyone in the industry would know it was up for grabs. Suddenly, the chances that I and my group of investors would prevail seemed slimmer than ever before.

Having come this far, however, Sam and I were determined to buy a company or group of companies in the foodservice area. Hearing that Alco Standard Corporation was interested in selling seven of its companies, we looked into buying them.

When I advised the Blodgett board of our proposal to buy the Alco companies, they asked me to take a leave of absence until negotiations with both companies were completed.

My departure from Blodgett coincided with problems of another kind. Our new house was not yet finished, and the lease on the house we had rented had expired.

As October 1988 dawned, I suddenly found myself without a company, temporarily without a job, without a home, and living with my family in a motel. What, indeed, had I done?

Ironically, the negotiations with Alco, which ultimately fell through, served to move Blodgett off the dime. Just when I was seriously wondering if I had indeed lost the throw of the dice, negotiations lurched forward. First Boston Corporation and Metropolitan Life were now in the picture, and Blodgett was finally willing to negotiate seriously for the first time.

On December 21, 1988, the contract to buy Blodgett was finally signed, and the company was renamed G.S. Blodgett Corporation.

Several months have now passed since that momentous day.

Looking back, there can be no doubt that the decision to buy Blodgett was the most agonizing of my life. It was also the most rewarding.

It certainly crystallized my thinking of how to conduct business on a day-to-day basis. Being something of a risk taker, the LBO experience, in a very *big* way, underscored what I've always believed: *To achieve goals of consequence,* it is necessary to assume some level of risk. It also confirmed something else I believed strongly: To be a winner it is important to hang tough and stay the course once it has been chosen.

While I was often concerned over temporary setbacks — and, I might add, surprised by the number of people rooting for me to fall on my face — I found great comfort in two things. First, I was sure of my goal. And secondly, I felt I had behaved honorably throughout. I was completely open with the board, shareholders, and other concerned parties, and my intentions of buying the company and reasons for doing so were always well known to them.

The months following the acquisition have, at times, been rough. Following the battle for control of the company morale was low, and many employees who had been with Blodgett for 30 years or more simply could not make the transition to the new team.

It has been an exhilarating time as well. We've had to do some streamlining including selling one company, and closing and merging another, but we've been careful to treat our people well and turn the transactions into win-win situations for everyone involved.

When we sold Wilder Manufacturing, a company we bought in 1986, for example, we made every effort to sell it back to its management and succeeded.

The struggle for Blodgett taught me a great deal personally and professionally. Perhaps the overriding lesson was it's who you do business with that counts. People are the key. I had great financial partners, particularly Sam, and a loyal staff who carried on during the negotiations with Blodgett. They stuck with it even when I was on leave and the company's future and theirs was in doubt, and they've dug in since the acquisition to make the *new* Blodgett a success.

A Leader Is An Educator

Allan Schuman is President of Ecolab Services Group, Ecolab, Inc., an organization engaged in the development and marketing of cleaning, sanitizing, pest and maintenance services for the hospitality, institutional, and food processing markets. He is a member of the Board of Directors of the International Foodservice Manufacturer's Association.

Question: How would you describe your management style, and why did you choose to adopt or develop it in that way?

I've read many descriptions of the management styles x, y and z and as far as I'm concerned those theories have nothing to do with successful management. The letters themselves don't mean much to me, and the theories seem an unnecessarily inflexible set of standards that are irrelevant to the constantly changing and mutable situation we deal in the world of business.

I don't look at management or leadership issues with a textbook "theory" in mind. And I would never try to lock myself or my employees into a "style" of behavior. If there's a method behind my management, it goes much deeper than style. I don't think a leader can be truly effective if he or she simply chooses and adapts trappings of style. Leadership stems from a lifetime approach to people.

You've got to have two attitudes bred or bled into you; you've got to learn these two attitudes yourself, or let the world teach them to you. (It hurts less the first way.)

  a) an overwhelming, all consuming, uncompromising, unwavering and relentless devotion to your customer — at all levels at any cost

  b) an intense awareness and participation in the activity

around you. A leader is not a narcissist. He or she doesn't have to be. A leader pays attention, always, and is always concocting a solution.

I've seen lots of people climb, and "succeed" but they can only get so far and only be so effective if their sights aren't set for the good of the company and the needs of their customers.

The devotion to customer is obvious to anyone who has come from a sales background, and many of us have, in some way or another. A good salesperson is always focused *outward* — keeping very close to the customer, observing, listening. And in business — whether marketing, budget planning, R&D, or public affairs — we are always selling something.

So we've all learned a basic precept: the customer comes first. And we are still learning how to keep that rule intact. If, as a business leader, you lose that focus, you're headed for trouble. Your office gets bigger, the leather softer, the windows wider, and it's tempting to forget where you came from, or how and why you got into that office in the first place. But if you do forget, you will no longer be able to lead.

I try to make sure that I never forget the proper focus — the customer. If a customer calls and asks for me — I take the call. I try to talk to as many food and beverage managers, stewards, and dish machine operators as I can. When I go out to eat, I always work my way back to the kitchen. That's where *my* customer is.

Our company has written a document called the "Quest for Excellence." It's more thorough than a mission statement, more crucial than an operating plan. We keep the "Quest" hanging on our office walls and in our elevators. We laminate it and send it to the sales field. We show it to our customers. In the "Quest," here's what we say about them:

> "The company that fails its customers fails. We will be superior to our competitors in providing the highest value to our customers at a fair price. We will constantly listen to our customers, respond quickly to their current needs, and anticipate future needs. We will stay close to our customers, tell them the truth, and earn their business every day."

That's not a management style; that's a vision. A company has to share a common vision to remain viable, challenged, and in a growth posture. I think have made my first point.

My second point, awareness and participation, is really about the human spirit — tapping in to yourself and those around you. If that is your goal, all issues of style will then fall into place.

I'm not talking abstractions here. What I'm talking about has nothing to do with theology, mysticism, or that which can't be seen. I have seen the very real effects of inner resources. Ask any salesperson what it is that makes him or her devote 24 hours a day to a customer. Greed will burn you out. Ego will burn you out. But 100 percent concern, devotion and loyalty — spirit — will take you a long way.

You've got to love your business. There's no reason not to. It's people, it's action, and it's interaction. Bring everything you have and everything you have done into your business dealings. I don't believe in half-measures in any part of life, least of all half-leadership or half-management. I bring to my business dealings my formal education, my "street smarts," my widespread reading and my volunteer experience and activities. Most of all, I bring a comprehensive understanding of all aspects of this industry. To make strategic decisions on our company's future, I need to know how other leaders in the restaurant and hotel business see their business and their future.

But even though I am 100 percent involved with this industry, both heart and soul, I know my limits. I only extend so far. I am not here to stretch my ego across the globe or see myself being strung out in sales districts across the country. A purely egotistical person doesn't function well in business. Internal power? Yes! Digging within for resources? Yes! Awareness of self? Yes! But knowing where you end and others begin is a true mark of leadership.

There is nothing more gratifying, uplifting, challenging or productive than to be instrumental in the growth and learning of others. I take my primary role as a leader to be that of an educator. And since the word "educate" literally means to draw out, from my colleagues I try to draw out all of the intelligence, courage, talent and conviction that I know they possess. When there's big hurdles to clear, I call on people to give a little more. And they do it. They sometimes give more than I had imagined possible. My greatest motivation is being able to motivate others. And my greatest success is when my educational leadership efforts bring success to others.

I am not a drill-master type teacher. I don't ask anyone to get up and write on the wall "I made a mistake" one hundred times. Mistakes can be used as guideposts. Cyberneticians use the obstacle as a means to set the course. So if you hit a roadblock, just get back on track.

But don't hit the same post twice. If you keep going back to the same roadblock for a daily knock on the head, you've got a problem. If others are hitting the same roadblocks repeatedly, and all you're doing in response is repeatedly pointing out those roadblocks, then you'll wind up with the same headache. When others make mistakes, point them out. Once, and with impact. After mistakes are made and noted, put them in the past. That's where they belong.

I am a taskmaster type teacher. I demand that those around me learn to solve their own problems, accomplish their own tasks. If they come to me stumped, I will simply repeat the facts back to them. Or if it's more complicated, I'll assemble the pieces into one, visible location so that all the necessary elements are present. Then it's up to the employee to point the pieces in the right direction, and fit those pieces together. It's a lot of work for them. That's good. The lessons you have to work out for yourself are the ones that will stick with you. They are the only ones you really learn well. And each lesson successfully taught brings the employee that much closer to success. They discover an intelligence and a synthetic, creative ability of their own. They realize that they've done something. They come to understand that they can do more.

Some people with big egos want to lay it all out themselves to show everyone how it all fits together. They want to prove that they're the mastermind, the person with all the answers. I realized early that such childish egotism advances no cause and helps no company. We don't click together as well as we do because we're a bunch of egos playing king of the mountain, nor do we work well because one person leads and the others follow. We're all talented, and I thrill from bringing that talent to the fore.

I learned this lesson in sales. An inexperienced salesperson wants to look smart. He or she goes to a customer with a speech prepared, all standard customer objections ready to be met. There's a presentation, a demonstration. Everything runs smoothly. And he or she pulls out his order form, expecting a sale.

But the sale isn't made. Why? Because while the salesperson was giving a canned presentation, the customer was distracted by his own problems. That salesperson didn't notice the customer's employees spilling liquid detergent on the floor, gumming up equipment with too much powder, or wasting time on unnecessary procedures. The customer did, however! You've got to notice what's going on in the room around you at all times, what the person you are working with needs. We observed that our customers needed a solid detergent. So we gave it to them. What your employees don't need is someone with all the answers. They need to discover those answers within themselves. That discovery will make them a success.

What motivates any good business manager and leader is success. My definition of that word is very broad. It most certainly includes the bottom line. But the best method of making that bottom line grow is by helping the entire company and everyone in it to succeed. As a leader, I open doors for people and then step aside. If they miss the entrance, I'll guide them through. That's cybernetics. If they're sluggish, I'll nudge them. That's motivation. If they learn that they can pass through that door and the many others beyond it, that's education. And with that kind of education, they will lead you and your business to success.

It's Management's Job *To Know*

Robert S. Wood is Vice Chairman of Bob Evans Farms, Inc. He is a Director of the National Restaurant Association.

Question: How would you describe your management style, and why did you choose to adopt or develop it in that way?

A 35 year career with Bob Evans Farms has helped me to develop my management and leadership style. In one sense it's difficult to distinguish between *my* leadership style and those qualities for which our company has become known, for we certainly share the same beginnings. My management style, therefore, is as much a reflection of our company culture as anything else.

It was while I was growing up in the rolling countryside of southeastern Ohio that I learned life's basic lessons. It was in this same part of rural America that our company got its start which was founded on those fundamental philosophies that middle America brought to work every day.

It seems to me that if you don't stand for something, you stand for nothing. We chose to do business the same way we have lived our lives, with honesty and integrity and treating people as we want to be treated. Sounds simple, doesn't it? Yet we've grown and prospered by setting our standards this way.

As I look back, I can see that my personal style of managing evolved from these same basic tenets. A pragmatic, ethical, common-sense approach has given me the ability to provide direction and focus for our people, simply by incorporating participative management — the value of sharing information with, and encouraging input from, others. I have to say I am proud of that, not only because of how far we've come and the accomplishments we've been able to achieve, but because of the possibilities for us based on that strength.

A thorough knowledge of the business is required to make the tough decisions every leader needs to make in order for his or her company to survive during trying times and excel at all other times. It is my belief that these decisions are made by using the information gained by totally involving yourself in the business. It takes time to visit restaurants, talk to employees, listen to customers, and study the competition; however, this involvement provides a person with the knowledge needed to evaluate options and opportunities.

It is my belief that this knowledge is an essential aspect of leadership. It is management's job *to know*. How else can you ask the right questions and provide the right direction? Only by understanding the business and the environment in which it exists can you consider the full range of opportunities. And only by understanding will you be able to accept the enormous responsibility of ensuring your company's ongoing success.

Cautious deliberation is deeply rooted in my upbringing. If you don't have very much to start with and you've worked hard to get what you have, you are certainly not going to risk losing it for any reason. The discipline of that thinking has become the cornerstone of our success.

As we grow and attract bright, talented, young people who bring their own expertise and experience to our business, it becomes a challenge to develop and strengthen their personal management style yet instill within them the traditions that have brought us this far. It is important to encourage sound decision-making without stifling the energy and enthusiasm that is necessary for them to lead us to greater heights in the future.

To summarize my management style, I believe that it can best be described as one of planning, organizing, directing, and caring. However, this style is supported by a firm foundation formed by hard work, commitment, logical thinking, and a practical application of knowledge.

You Can't Enjoy Success
Without Experiencing Failure

Walter J. Conti is Owner/Manager of the award winning Conti Cross Keys Inn located in Doylestown, Pennsylvania. He is an IFMA Gold Plate Award winner and is past President of the National Restaurant Association.

Question: From a personal perspective, how do you handle success and overcome disappointments?

The question is an interesting one. I don't think you can have one without the other as success and disappointment serve as measuring rods for one another. Both success and disappointment are a way of life for anyone who is involved in the day-to-day activities of the hospitality industry.

How to handle success is the more difficult part of the question. I have known people with sizable egos who seem consumed by success in that their every thought and action is geared to impress on others how successful they are. Some people talk a lot about their success rather than letting others talk about it. Some people worry that others won't think of them as successful or worry about how long their success will last.

Some successful people are not particularly successful in *managing* their own success. They want others to envy them, they make dramatic changes in their lifestyle and habits, and change the way they relate to and interact with others.

I think that truly successful people are those who possess an inner security that causes them not to think of themselves as being particularly successful. They don't think of themselves as being unsuccessful, but they retain the basic values, standards, lifestyle, and demeanor that always gave definition to their own identity. They are psychologically comfortable with themselves.

Controlling one's actions and solving day-to-day problems are all part of living successfully. I've often wondered what successful people think when their operation is running smoothly. This is the most critical time of one's professional life. It's always easier to fix or refine a wheel than it is to build a wheel. I suspect successful people are never satisfied. I think they keep looking to make things better and to undertake new challenges. I think they work hard to maintain the disciplines that caused them to be succesful. I also think they keep abreast of what their customers want, and treat their employees with the dignity they deserve.

Overcoming disappointment can be easier, for you simply have to do it. There is no other acceptable alternative. You know that disappointments will occur. You may not know what specifically will be involved, but everyone experiences disappointments, so expect them. It's all a part of life.

Disappointment serves a positive purpose. It brings us back to reality. It represents a challenge that we must hurdle. It's disciplining, for it gives us a resolve that we might not otherwise exercise.

Experience can be helpful in overcoming disappointment as it gives us a confidence that we can manage whatever it is that caused the disappointment. Sometimes it's necessary to rely on outside people to assist you as they can often look at the situation more objectively as they bring a different perspective to the environment. Once you realize that you *can* overcome disappointment, then you *must* overcome it.

Overall, you can't really understand the concept of success without understanding the concept of failure. Success gives us the confidence, strength, and ability to overcome disappointment. Disappointment is character building which leads to resolve and confidence and that, in turn, can lead to success.

Expect Success,
Manage Disappointments

Robert D. Flickinger is the Retired Chairman, CEO, and co-founder of Service Systems Corporation, a contract management services organization located in Buffalo, New York, now owned by the Marriott Corporation. He is past President of the National Restaurant Association.

Question: From a personal perspective, how do you handle success and overcome disappointments?

Success takes on different meanings at different levels of growth and development. In the beginning, it's what you are working toward as an individual, in terms of doing your job to the best of your ability in reaching the immediate goals and objectives that are before you. The actual accomplishment of those goals and objectives and the sense of satisfaction and confidence that accompanies it causes one to grow in both perspective and expectations. We always expected success both personally and organizationally and never thought about or considered failure as a possibility. Hard work and smart work simply elevated the level of success we felt and which was demonstrated as the company grew in size and profitability. We were never content to remain in place, we were always reaching for the next level of expansion. We realized early on that we could not stagnate as a company and expect to survive, let alone prosper in the long run. The marketplace is a dynamic, not a static environment, and if you think you're standing still, in reality, you are slipping backward. From that perspective success is a continuing process, not a fixed state of being.

We encountered disappointments, setbacks, and roadblocks along the way to be sure, but we knew that this was part of the process of growth and the problems that arose were there to be managed and solved. We regarded problems as temporary. There was nothing we could not overcome in some way, whether it was a business issue, a personnel matter, an interface with government agencies, or what have you. We had a lot of good things happen and, of course, we had somethings that went the other way. These were good learning processes for us as they narrowed the range of our emotions. We never got too elated over our successes to the degree that we took anything for granted. By the same token, we never got too depressed over the disappointments we experienced, they just strengthened our resolve to persevere and to go on. From that vantage point, I think success is the ability to take things in stride so that your behavior and perhaps your lifestyle doesn't change so markedly as to cause you to become a different type of person than what made you successful in the first place.

As the company continued to grow, we made some business acquisitions and also had opportunities to connect with other firms. In 1967, we felt it was the right thing for the company, as part of the continuing process, to sell to the Del Monte Corporation. That occurred in early 1968. Not only did we consider it from a business point of view, we also considered it from a people point of view. We felt it was the right thing for our people as well, so that they could participate in the success of the company to which they had contributed so much.

From that perspective then, success has meaning in the context of people sharing in the positive developments of what they help foster.

When success is manifested in terms of moderate or considerable wealth, people expect you to be more of a financial contributor to the industry from which you came, to the community in which you live, and the society of which you are a part. This is a normal expectation on their part, and they attribute and measure your success in large part by the level of your participation with them. That aspect of success has to be managed carefully as well.

In summary, my answer to handling success is to do so with humility, poise, dignity and respect, and to realize that disappointments represent somewhat expected temporary challenges that can be addressed and surmounted.

The Harder You Work The Luckier You Become

Carl N. Karcher is Founder, Chairman of the Board, and Chief Executive Officer of Carl Karcher Enterprises, a major regional quick service chain headquartered in Anaheim, California. He is a recipient of the Horatio Alger award and was the MUFSO man of the year in 1983.

Question: From a personal perspective, how do you handle success and overcome disappointments?

When people ask me what it takes to handle success and overcome disappointment, I'm always reminded of an often repeated response: "Nobody ever said it was going to be easy."

And, quite frankly, I'm not sure that, in the final analysis, success is any easier to live with than disappointment. Don't get me wrong. Success is always more enjoyable to experience, but if it isn't handled and controlled properly, it can cause more grief than most disappointments. There are too many stories of people who have fallen from the pinnacle of success for that statement to be disputed.

I like to tell the story of how my wife, Margaret, and I started with just a single hot dog cart on a street corner in Los Angeles, how we bought it with a $311 loan on our automobile and added $15 of our own cash to complete the purchase, and how today, 48 years later, it has grown to more than 500 restaurants doing over $500,000,000 in sales per year.

That's the success part of the story. But understand that at no time did we ever sit back and think that we had finally "arrived," that we knew all there was to know about the business, or that we still didn't have to work as hard as we did on that very first day.

That's probably the key to handling success. Recognize it, be grateful for it, and probably live a little better because of it. But don't ignore the attendant responsibilities. Success always means more obligations, to your community that is providing the atmosphere that allows the opportunities for success and to your employees without whom you would have accomplished nothing.

Now isn't it interesting that I've talked about success without even attempting to define it. I won't either, because that's a never ending game, and I'm not sure we can all agree on what success is. From my standpoint I've never regarded success as a destination. Rather, I've always regarded it as a journey, and I'm sure that attitude has helped me keep whatever success has come my way in proper perspective.

So much for the handling of success. Now, what about that thing we seem to experience much more often, disappointment?

I tell the story of the hot dog cart because it always seems to excite people with the unrecognized opportunities that surround them. Perhaps I should also tell them about the time, a few weeks after the purchase, when we were almost closed down because the business we bought owed back taxes.

They weren't ours but we had to pay them.

I could also tell about the person I hired to run the cart while I was working on my bread route. He soon figured out a way to take money without me knowing it. Had I not caught him he would have put me out of business. Talk about a disappointment!

There have been a number of other disappointments through the years, a few of which stand out more than others, but these are simply representative of the rest. We bought a chain of coffee shops and never could get them to show a profit. We followed the expensive advice of some very highly regarded consultants and opened up a new fast food concept. It almost broke us. We opened a number of restaurants in other areas and in a few years had to close all of them to the tune of a $15,000,000 write off. And, finally, there continue to be people who abuse the trust we place in them and who have to be terminated. Perhaps those are the greatest disappointments of all.

Now, through all of this, what have I learned about handling success and disappointment? One of my few regrets is that I haven't seemed to find time to read as much as I should like. So much can be learned from the wisdom of others. But I do remember reading the poem "IF" by Rudyard Kipling. In it there is a line that has since been carved over the fireplace at Wimbledon in England, and I think it about says it all regarding the subject:

> "If you can meet with Triumph and Disaster, and treat
> those two imposters just the same;"

You see, more often than not our greatest successes and our most disastrous disappointments become such largely because of the opinions of others and because we let the opinions of others influence our own. Almost without exception, success and failure (disappointment) are largely transitory. Often times the most important things we do are completely unknown to others, and we simply contend with them as normal events of the day.

Now if we were to take these secret successes and disappointments and expose them to the world for the world's opinion of them, we would be on an emotional roller coaster that would completely wear us out in a week. As it is, we experience great successes and withstand terrible disappointments and do so with great strength because the world doesn't tell us that one thing is good and the other thing bad. When all is said and done we are the master of our own lives. We alone can decide whether or not ours will be a happy and productive life, regardless of the circumstances. Success and disappointment, like triumph and disaster, are too often imposters that other people impose on us. We forget that neither is permanent.

I was very fortunate to have the parents I did. Without ever authoring a book or writing a list of rules both of them, by example and occasional admonition, taught all of us children some very basic fundamentals of life. We learned early in life that, "The harder you work, the luckier you become;" "The word can't died in the poorhouse;" "Watch your pennies and the dollars will take care of themselves;" and "Never lose faith in the divine providence of God."

Success and disappointment are with us all through life. They are like fire and water. We need them both and can't do without either. The important thing is to let neither of them become our master.

Successful Subordinates Are An Achievement, Not A Threat

Max Pine is President and Chief Executive Officer of Restaurant Associates Industries Inc., a diversified foodservice firm headquartered in New York City.

Question: From a personal perspective, how do you handle success and overcome disappointments?

Success, like beauty, is in the eye of the beholder. Different people will always measure success differently. I believe that one of the major measures of success for anyone running an organization is the success that his or her people achieve. If you have selected people for positions at which they have proven successful, then that is your success just as much as if you had done it yourself. Actually, it's a more important success because you've created a talented team. Applaud their success. Never allow yourself to view them as a threat.

Success offers a wonderful reason for celebration. But that celebration should not just be for yourself, it should include all of those people in the organization that brought about that success. Sometimes you have to make yourself stop and think about which people contributed to the success and make sure that they are all recognized and participate in the celebration.

There is a dangerous aspect to success. You have to avoid becoming overconfident, cocky, and complacent as a result of success. You should examine why each success occurred. What did you really do to make it happen? You have to isolate those factors that made a difference and caused that success so you will have a chance of repeating it.

In every successful situation there are serendipitous factors, as well as the ones which you caused to happen. You have to devote the necessary time to analyze what happened in order to know what you did right. It's an opportunity to learn, to gain insight and understanding that may contribute to the next success.

The more you experiment, strive to do better, and expand your business, the more likely failure and disappointment will occur. Also, the higher your standards, the more disappointments you're going to experience. Disappointments need to be recognized and brought out in the open, otherwise the organization won't be able to benefit from them. Depending on the nature of the disappointment, learn from it the same way you learn from success. Analyze it and don't blame others when it's your fault. Although you want to be realistic, it does help to try to find a positive side to any disappointment. The easiest thing is to think that "it could have been worse." People prefer being on a winning team, but that doesn't mean you shouldn't acknowledge disappointments. If you bury your disappointments, if you hide your mistakes, the likelihood is greater that they will be repeated. Also, you're not being honest and you're not communicating.

Unless failure can be talked about openly in an organization, risk-taking won't come easily. Every success or disappointment that is shared is a way of making the people around you understand your vision and aspirations for yourself and your organization. That builds trust, and trust is a major building block for a successful organization.

Capitalize On Change
Or You'll Go Out With It

Shannon Talley is President and Chief Executive Officer of Com-Source Independent Foodservice Companies, Inc., headquartered in Atlanta, Georgia, which provides 140 independent foodservice member distributors with cooperative procurement and marketing programs. He is a 1989 recipient of the International Foodservice Manufacturers Association's (IFMA) Spark Plug award.

Question: From a personal perspective, how do you handle success and overcome disappointments?

I'm a builder. And, as with anything that is built, you begin with a vision and follow that with a strong foundation. I believe it is the strength of the foundation which will determine the outcome — regardless of what is being built. While I don't build houses or office buildings, a solid foundation is just as essential for success in the foodservice industry as it is in the construction field.

In fact, success in any field must be founded on a solid and dependable belief in yourself and your capabilities. You must believe you can succeed in order to do so, but that doesn't mean you stop there. Success is continually trying. Without the willingness to try, you'll never experience the excitement of success or the opportunity that comes from failure.

And that's the way I feel about failure. It really is an opportunity — an opportunity to succeed. Now, maybe that success won't be the way you originally planned, but you succeeded nevertheless. At one point in my career, I owned a food brokerage business. I worked at that brokerage company for two and a half years with some success, yet I never took it to the heights I thought it would go. I analyzed it, decided I didn't like that side of the business, and sold it. If I could do it over again, I

117

wouldn't buy that business in the first place. I succeeded by not living forever with a business I didn't enjoy. I learned some valuable lessons and I opened myself up to new opportunity.

When I started in foodservice, it wasn't even classified as an industry. And the only prerequisite for success, then as now, was a knowledge of your own capabilities — in one word, confidence. You must have the confidence to take advantage of the opportunities that exist. I once knew a young man who was truly brilliant. He was involved in the computer industry and was offered a rare and fabulous opportunity which he declined. The reason: lack of inner confidence. Now, I promise you that I am not brilliant — intelligent, yes, but I wouldn't classify myself as brilliant. Yet when I finished college and took over my father's frozen food locker plant in 1951, one of the first things I did was raise my salary from $300 to $400 a month. Even though I needed $400 per month, my mother was still horrified! But I knew I hadn't raised my salary on a whim. I knew my primary motivation for working wasn't to pad my wallet but to create, to build something of value. And, I had the inner confidence to know that I was worthy of $400 a month, that I was going to do what was necessary to bring in enough revenue to support my new salary. While inner confidence does grow with achievement, I think you must have a rock-solid foundation of confidence, of belief in yourself, to build upon. You must trust yourself.

But you can't be cocky. A little humility will get you much farther than over-confidence any day of the week. If you sit around and enjoy a success too long, there probably won't be another success to enjoy. Success is short-lived. It is fleeting. Actually, success is a series of plateaus or events. If you stop working hard and setting objectives, you can no longer obtain success, nor will you continue to be successful — in your eyes or in the eyes of others. I can tell you for a fact that my Board of Directors doesn't care what I accomplished last year, they only care about what I will achieve this year. That's as it should be.

And just as success is a fleeting, short-lived event, so should disappointment be. Failure is usually a series of minor incidents rather than something monumental. And, it is by failing and analyzing that failure that we develop most of our skills. Failure is a great opportunity to learn. By the same token, if you have too many of these educational opportunities, you'll probably lose your money or your job!

We all make mistakes. It's how we deal with those mistakes that matters. Mistakes are usually an indication of poor judgment, not poor ability. No one is exempt from making poor decisions. And, although I may occasionally doubt a decision I've made, I never doubt my ability.

Let's say a mistake has been made, an objective has met with failure — which is really just a temporary set back. The important thing is what happens next. ComSource is a collective procurement company owned by 140 Members. If it weren't for our Members, we wouldn't exist. So, it really hurts when we lose a Member. Not too long ago, we lost a Member whose geographic market share will never be replaced. That was a major disappointment. I admit that the first thing you do is feel downright sick for a few hours, but then you step back and objectively analyze the situation. This particular loss was both unavoidable and uncontrollable. There was nothing I could do to regain that geographic market share. But, we could compensate for the loss of revenue, and it was my job to set an objective to do just that. We either had to cut costs or replace the lost Member. We replaced the Member. One disappointment brought about another success. You must be able to deal with disappointment, to cope with it, in order to succeed. Very often, once you analyze a mistake, a failure, or a disappointment, you see it from a different angle and have the opportunity to build from it.

In reality, both success and failure are all in your mind. You can't succeed unless you think you can, and you can only fail if you think you will. Your attitude will determine your outcome.

Attitude is the most important thing. You must be positive, you must believe in yourself, and you must be confident. But you must also be willing to change, to adapt, and to grow. The foodservice industry is not a stagnant one. It is constantly changing because it is still growing. You must be able to capitalize on change or you will go out with change. If I didn't think of myself as a builder, if I didn't realize the importance of creating and expanding, of growth and opportunity, then I would probably be a spectator in the stands watching others succeed. Instead, I'm playing an active role in creating a new business, implementing new concepts, and even shaping the growth of an industry.

Opportunity does not come without risk. It is impossible to succeed or fail without taking a few chances. But these chances should be calculated ones. If a risk is so great that its failure could close your doors, then it is certainly not worth taking. Each risk should be carefully weighed. At one time, we used a food broker. This broker warehoused product, took orders from distributors, and then shipped product to those distributors. I thought this was nonsense. Why should we pay someone a fee to do something we could do better ourselves? We decided to purchase product and warehouse it ourselves. This was definitely a calculated risk because it was an untried, unproven idea. Both financial and professional risks were inherent in this venture, but I put myself on the line for this idea because I was convinced that it would work. It did! That one idea became the foundation for that company. In less than a year it was both successful and profitable. In fact, our success affected the prevailing trend in the industry. Many other companies have changed their direction as a result. Now, collective procurement is both the foundation and the primary purpose of ComSource. One idea, one vision, built a business, but only because I was willing to take a calculated risk.

In fact, had I not taken that risk, I couldn't have achieved what I believe is my greatest success, the merger of NIFDA and North American Companies to form ComSource.

I didn't achieve that success or any success alone. I have an excellent staff. We all have a common goal which we work together to achieve. I also have a confidant. I believe a confidant is essential to both success and disappointment. My confidant is my wife. She is always there to help me brainstorm for ideas, keep disappointments in perspective, and celebrate the successes.

Convert Breakdowns Into Breakthroughs

S.J. DiMeglio is President and Chief Executive Officer of Guest Services, a diversified foodservice firm based at Fairfax, Virginia.

Question: What is your most memorable business experience, and what did you learn from it?

Several years ago I was working with the Fred Harvey Company as General Manager of the La Fonda Hotel in Santa Fe, New Mexico. The incident I'm relating here occurred during the month of August, the height of the "season" in Santa Fe. On one particular Saturday night the hotel was filled to capacity. The level of activity in the lobby was such that my front desk personnel were kept running, and I had come from my office to oversee the business of welcoming and registering our guests.

Lo and behold, into the midst of the commotion a bus load of tourists arrived, forty tired, hungry people ready to relax in our comfortable accommodations. The tour guide presented the booking slip for twenty rooms, but as we initiated the registration process, we discovered that these particular reservations had not been recorded in our books!

We were faced with a potential catastrophe. The hotel and the city were filled to capacity. I had no idea where there were twenty rooms to be found to accommodate 40 increasingly anxious people. Those people standing in my lobby who had every right and reason to expect that they would be welcomed at our hotel had made their reservations well in advance and were simply the unwitting victims of a system breakdown utterly beyond their control. In addition, I represented an exceptionally honorable, ethical company. It was my duty to remedy an error, salvage our reputation, and prevent an unfortunate circumstance from deteriorating into a crisis.

I had confirmed earlier information that there were no rooms available in Santa Fe. The nearest location having accommodations on a comparable level with ours was Albuquerque, some 60 miles to the south. Fred Harvey's Alvarado hotel in Albuquerque was completely booked. The Hilton, fortunately, had rooms available, and I was able to negotiate a reasonable rate. I then arranged a complimentary dinner for the group at the Alvarado, our hotel in Albuquerque.

Despite the inconvenience of an unplanned trip to Albuquerque and the general confusion created by the situation, I later received letters from the tour leader and several members of the group indicating how much they enjoyed the "side trip" as it added to their adventure. Dinner had been a great success and their accommodations were entirely satisfactory.

A couple of valuable lessons came out of that memorable experience that I have never forgotten. The first is that customer service and satisfaction is paramount in the hospitality business. The Fred Harvey Company made many more friends than enemies that evening, which goes to show that people are reasonable and truly appreciative of kindness when they face adversity. The necessary extra effort on our part compensated for the disappointment and frustration those ladies and gentlemen felt when they found there was "no room at our inn." I think it says a lot about the power of positive thinking and a positive attitude.

The second important lesson is that I always look at the possibility of turning a breakdown into a breakthrough. By dint of effort, oftentimes a disaster can become a diversion and then a delight. Our would-have-been guests experienced a richer, more fruitful journey than they would otherwise have known, including a complimentary dinner. In going a step further and considering options outside the parameters of the ordinary, I stretched the boundaries of my thinking. The stretch felt so good I decided to make it a habit. Everyone I connect with benefits, and when they also get in the groove of unfettered thinking, good things happen. Try it!

Heroes Are Not Always Celebrities

Florence Jaramillo is Owner/Manager of Rancho De Chimayo, an award winning restaurant in Chimayo, New Mexico. She is a member of the Board of Directors of the National Restaurant Association.

Question: Who are (or were) your heroes and heroines in life, and why do you think of them in that light?

I have had a number of heroes and heroines in my life but I'll mention only six of them here as they stand out in my mind as giving something to me, and to others I am sure, that is priceless, and valued beyond imagination. This question caused me to take a trip down memory lane and as I thought about my heroes anew, I realized even more fully just how helpful they have been to me. I am a better person because of their care, concern, sincerity, and friendship.

At a very early age, Mary Seidman, the owner of a small neighborhood grocery store took me under her wing and taught me the virtue of responsibility. She showed me how to make change from a cash register, how to shop carefully, how to identify good produce, and how to get the best buys. I was a very young girl, and she treated me as an adult. I never forgot that.

The principal of my grade school, Sister Carmelita, instilled in me the importance and the love of education. Although I was not the brightest student, she took the time to help me and to make sure that I retained what I had learned. She stressed thoroughness and attention to details, qualities which have served me well over the years.

In my teens, one of my best friend's mother, Sophie LaPorte, taught me the social graces. I was invited to accompany their family to various outings such as going to the theatre and visiting restaurants where I learned about a whole new world. She introduced me to a culture that I had not experienced before, and I was transformed from a girl into a young woman.

For 12 years of my life, my first major employer, Frank Blesso, taught me that you can do anything in life if you work hard, have an open mind, really listen, and recognize that learning is a life long process. He taught me to develop a vision and to seek it. The difference between a dreamer and a visionary is action. Dreamers dream, visionaries do it.

W.D. Peterson, an accountant in Santa Fe, New Mexico, taught me self-confidence through his confidence in me. I was unsure of myself and my abilities but he encouraged me to keep moving ahead, to keep growing, to keep developing.

Another restaurateur, Mrs. Dolly Barge, taught me involvement and the importance of being part of your community. She introduced me to the concept that your experience of life should be greater than your business environment.

The whole of life extends well beyond your property boundaries and when you recognize that others can benefit from what you offer to them it adds a new dimension to being human.

Most of these people were immigrants who succeeded in their own endeavors, but fortunately they took an interest in me at a time in my life when their guidance and assistance really made a difference.

I know that anyone reading this will not recognize the names of my heroes and heroines for they are not industry household names. I think that for many of us that's the nature of things, i.e., our true heroes and heroines are the ones who reach us personally in some way. They are not celebrities; they don't receive much if any public recognition. They don't even think of themselves as someone's hero or heroine. But they are!

Five Simple Lessons

Michael E. Hurst is Owner/Manager of the 15th Street Fisheries in Ft. Lauderdale, Florida. He also serves as a Professor at Florida International University. He is the 1990/91 Vice President of the National Restaurant Association.

Question: What is your most memorable business experience, and what did you learn from it?

Very early in my career I was fortunate to meet Ed Mirvish who then owned Honest Ed's department store in Toronto. He gave me a book written about him called *Business Is People* which had a profound impact on me and the direction I would take in my career.

The book wasn't a scholarly work, never got reviewed by the *New York Times* nor made any list of anything, and probably more were given away than sold. The book was based on experiences that didn't relate to the hospitality industry. It was the reflection of a man who had achieved phenomenal business success due to his focus on people.

People are an important part of the hospitality industry. While that isn't anything new, I often think of Ed Mirvish and the lessons learned from him as they have added up for me in this business. In my career, I have watched our industry lose sight of this perspective only to rediscover it anew as society forces us to do so.

We are consumer driven and suddenly our focus is back to the customer and more particularly to the staff that serves our customers.

I have five memorable experiences that I want to share with you.

I learned the importance of customers on my first job. I was twelve years old and washing glasses. I couldn't keep up although I was working as fast as I could. It took me two hours longer than I was scheduled. Once I was done, I was apologizing to my supervisor. I asked how many customers we had and found that we broke the record, almost 200 more than forecast. I was a winner! And I was playing on a winning team! My whole life I've kept that focus because my employees and I keep it there. Tonight and tomorrow, over and over, how many did we do? Did we break the record? The target is customers.

The second lesson was taught to me by Paul Shank at the Tiffin Inn in Denver. His concept was to deliver food with food runners to get the product to the guests hotter and faster. This was 30 years before computers and remote ordering. I asked Paul if he thought the system accounted for his success. Nope — his success was because he managed for customers. This was but one little thing that made the food come out hotter or colder and faster. His management for customers made so much sense twenty years later when I had an opportunity to do the same thing. By shifting the work around I, too, had a delivery system. The lesson I learned twice is that work must be done, but customers value service more highly. Provide more service and you create customers.

The third lesson was taught to me by Win Schuler. I learned that dining out was a total experience and that people were buying a pleasant experience. That included recognition and friendliness and helping them have fun. Win was a genius at all of them. From the greeting to the goodbye and the good food in between, he proved over and over his philosophy of "giving to get." It's easy to say those words. They don't mean much until you see all the little unexpected things that can be done to make the dining experience more pleasant. I learned that money expended to sell my present customer was worth far more than any spent trying to create a new customer. From remembering names to special tables, from lovers salads to special appetizers and desserts, the philosophy of "giving to get" meant exceeding customers expectations.

At about the time of lesson three, it seemed that the public developed a love affair with food. During a trip to Australia, an unusual dish appeared on the menu of the Coral Trout Restaurant in Brisbane. I was there with part of my family and when we saw Moreton Bay Bugs on the menu, we knew they were for us. It turned out they tasted like lobster. What fun! With a seafood restaurant in Florida, there couldn't be a more perfect place in the world to sell Bugs. Most Floridians would think we had discovered a new low food cost dish, Palmetto Bugs, the American Cockroach of Florida.

Samples were given away for several years and we asked people to guess what it was and whether we should put them on the menu. They were amazed to learn about Bugs and the story behind them. It became fun for everyone, our service staff and the customer. It was so much fun that out of a 75 item menu, this became the number three best seller, year in and year out. The lesson here is that food is fun. The customer is willing to try tasty, unusual items if we just introduce them in the right way. Next time they will buy it because fun is precious at any price.

The fifth lesson I put together myself. It was a product of a lot of years in the business. It occurred in flashes but never really firmed up until I had my own place. I realized by then that the customer was important, but I suddenly saw that the most important people to me were my front of the house/guest contact people. All the rest of us were supporters in making them look great. With that in mind, the internal focus had to be first on recruitment and selection, but then more importantly, on making the work exciting and fun. The whole thing couldn't be labor. The guest experience was determined by the staff performance and that was geared to the way I directed them. Service was and is the highest level of competition in the hospitality industry. Giving away the gift of friendship is as important or even more so than the good food, the decor, etc. The lesson I took so long to learn is that the greatest compliment I can get is, "Where do you get the nice people who work here?"

Five simple lessons — all summed up in a book title, *Business Is People*. No matter who wrote it first, it's the lesson of the hospitality industry. From the lessons of yesterday comes my game plan for tomorrow, *Business is People*.

Customers Don't Always Equal Profits

Harris O. Machus is Chairman Emeritus of Harris O. Machus Enterprises Inc., headquartered in Birmingham, Michigan. He is a past president of the National Restaurant Association.

Question: What is your most memorable business experience, and what did you learn from it?

Unlike many, I never planned to be in the foodservice industry. My father and mother owned and operated a small retail bakery in Birmingham, Michigan, but I never had any intention of making bread and pastries my life. I left the family business for college and the pursuit of an entirely different career.

My father's unexpected death, however, altered my professional path. Uncertainly, I took over the family bake shop. Standing behind the old familiar counter and offering the delicious and familiar products I was not content. My home town of Birmingham, like my dreams, had changed. The trend of families moving out of the city and into suburbs was in progress. New retail shops were springing up on every corner. Our small bake shop stood in the center of it all.

Eager for a new challenge, I considered the need for a tearoom type of restaurant in our community. I began to sketch out my plans. Thus it was with a great deal of enthusiasm and an even greater lack of critical knowledge, that I decided to expand and add a restaurant.

Looking back, I am certain that the phrase "ignorance is bliss" was never uttered by a profitable owner/operator in the foodservice industry.

My first business venture is memorable for many reasons. It was exciting. It was demanding. But most of all, it was personally and financially dangerous. In just a few short months my "new challenge" came very close to destroying my security. Failure loomed as my business seemed poised for disaster.

It is this particularly fatal and common circumstance that I'd like to share with you. Perhaps a focus on why I came close to failure and how I was able to correct the problem may be beneficial to you.

Our plans for expansion started well enough. We hired an architect, a builder, and an interior designer. We remodeled the bake shop and added a 90 seat restaurant. It was planned and designed for ladies and luncheons. In the afternoon we would feature pastries from our bake shop, as well as ice cream sundaes and sodas.

The first Machus restaurant was sensational to view. The carpet was pink. The table tops were pink formica. The chair seats and backs had pink fabric and black lacquered frames.

A young, knowledgeable, and handsome chef was hired. He was to prepare a variety of beautiful salads and scrumptious sandwiches in view of the ladies. His crisp, white uniform, neckerchief, and tall white hat made him look like a star from a Hollywood movie.

The stage was set. The curtain went up and when it did, our tearoom was a smashing success! Ladies were pleased and told their friends about the Machus restaurant and its convenience to downtown shops. Sales volume in our Machus bake shop increased as customers were tempted to purchase additional delights from our bakery display as they entered and exited the restaurant. In fact, customer count increased so heavily that we were forced to extend our luncheon through the afternoon. I was thrilled at our popularity. The food was great! The atmosphere, perfect! The location, ideal! And the profits, much to my horror and surprise, did not exist. We weren't making any money. In fact, we were losing.

Each week became more difficult financially. I was frantic. Our restaurant was filled with happy patrons yet we were coasting rapidly toward bankruptcy, and I didn't know why. Most importantly, I didn't know how to turn the problem around.

Luckily, I became aware of some evening classes on restaurant cost accounting. Some of our suppliers had mentioned that classes were being sponsored jointly by the National Restaurant Association and the Michigan Restaurant Association. I nearly rushed into the classroom. One highly qualified instructor and three classes later, my eyes were opened. I had been ill prepared to enter the restaurant business. My strategy for success had been based on a palatable menu, attractive interior, and novice enthusiasm. Quickly I was to learn that ours is a business of figures and percentages. Not even the best pastry and colorful interiors can turn a profit without a clear understanding of that fact.

Restaurant cost accounting taught me a vast array of business essentials. For example, how to "cost out" the price of every item on a plate/entree, and thus, price the entree properly. The importance of portion size and control. I became aware of waste and how little things add up to large expenses. For example, we used to peel potatoes by hand. Depending upon how thick/thin you peeled them, you were left with a certain amount of potato waste. I discovered that there were many examples of this invisible bandit in my business.

Unless you hire an experienced and precise bartender, for example, "free pouring" drinks are less cost effective than mixing/measuring. In general, restaurant cost accounting showed me the value of food/liquor control. Make no mistake. Keeping accurate records of food received, prepared, wasted, or stolen is vital to success.

For the next several months, I immersed myself in restaurant educational courses. Increased knowledge helped me to feel confident and make better decisions. I made continual changes in our daily procedures. I applied the techniques and advice shared with me by business veterans. Slowly, the P&L's from our CPA firm revealed a restaurant moving towards a healthy and profitable operation.

For years I attended classes, round table discussions, lectures, and seminars during the National Restaurant Association Trade Show in Chicago. Our Machus bake shop and restaurant became the talk of the community. Business flourished and profits were steady.

Over the years we expanded the restaurant several times to reach 150 seats and added a liquor service. Best of all, we have continued to grow.

Today, we have a staff of approximately 825. Our three prestigious free standing restaurants have received recognition through the Travel Holiday, Ivy, and Ford Times Awards. Our three casual restaurants and one elegant cafeteria thrive. And the little bake shop that started it all has blossomed into three renowned pastry shops.

My business philosophy has always been: "The quality of the food and service will be remembered long after the price is forgotten."

However, since my first brush with possible foodservice failure, my business practice has centered around procedure, detailed planning, stringent evaluation, and continuous control.

My recommendation to the foodservice operator of the future? First, expand your knowledge and experience. Take advantage of the many courses/lectures/seminars available. Obtain varied on-the-job experience. Read applicable materials. Ask lots of questions.

Secondly, consider a policy and procedure for everything within your operation. From what you expect of your employees to how you conduct food preparation, you should have set standards. More importantly, once standards are established, you need to insure that they are met. Our Machus Operational Manual (M.O.M.) is over 600 pages in length. I firmly believe that M.O.M. guidelines have been the cornerstone to our success.

Thirdly, remember that your employees are a direct reflection of your business image. A detailed evaluation of their "stage appearance" (In this industry we are always performing for our customers!), product knowledge, efficient service, and appropriate attitude is important.

At Machus, we've found that intense training, creative incentives, and fair pay help morale. Moreover, these items pay for themselves in quality customer service and employee job satisfaction.

I never "planned" to be a member of the foodservice industry. Luckily, I learned in the nick of time that "planning" is everything. After all, without knowledge, experience, and a solid blueprint for success, your money, time and energy may turn out to be just like a good Machus pastry — a long time in the making, but consumed in the blink of an eye.

Never Take Anyone, Or Anything, For Granted

Ernie and Willa Royal are proprietors of Ernie's Grill & Bar, Royal's Hearthside in Rutland, Vermont, where they have been in business for over a quarter of a century. Ernie Royal is an Honorary Director of the National Restaurant Association.

Question: What is your most memorable business experience, and what did you learn from it?

Willa and I have had many memorable experiences in the food-service industry, and to answer your question truly, we have to avoid the temptation to consider our most recent experience as the most indelible.

If we had to capsulize what we have learned from nearly half a century of work in, and love of, this industry it would be a two part principle. First, never, never, never take the customer for granted! The second part is a corollary to the first. Never, never, never take your employees for granted! Let us explain.

When we bought our first restaurant in 1955, we both had over 20 years of foodservice industry experience behind us, most of it in the Boston area which is known for its demanding restaurant customers. That early experience gave us the self-confidence and determination to open our own place of business with the $1500 we had saved over the years. We bought a three booth, seven counter seat restaurant in the Codman Square area of Boston. We operated that so successfully that we felt we were ready for bigger things, and an opportunity opened up for us to go to Rutland, Vermont, to open a restaurant. We grew the operation to a 265 seat establishment and added a side gourmet food and deli operation. The years were good to us, and in the early 1980's we thought it was time to sell the business and step out to smell the roses that grew outside the restaurant for a change. This is where the first part

133

of our "most memorable experience" begins.

Shortly after we sold out, the new owners discovered that they did not really like the restaurant business. Simultaneously, we rediscovered that we loved it and missed it, so it did not take much to get us back, albeit on a smaller scale. We knew that the reputation of the restaurant had suffered in the interim, and since the previous owners had retained our name, Royal's Hearthside, we felt we had to do something different but still keep whatever advantage there was to the old name. We decided to add the name "Ernie" to the old name, assuming customers, old and new, knew who Ernie was. Maybe some did but a whole lot more didn't, for it didn't give us the boost we hoped for. We downsized the scale of our operation to improve the product, and, of course, we expected customers to adjust to that change. Now being a smaller restaurant than before, we altered the entrance of the building from main street to another part of the building. Since the building had been in the same place for 26 years, we didn't think customers would have any trouble finding the door. Some did, but some didn't. In addition to these changes we also violated our rule of thumb of having one parking space for every two seats in the restaurant. When there is little or no foot traffic, adequate parking is essential to success. We took it for granted that customers would find a way to get to us. The first principle of never taking the customer for granted is what we've had to relearn these past three years. Seldom does a customer make a fuss when he or she does not like something or understand something that you may like and understand. More often than not, customers just quietly go someplace else. They register their displeasure with their feet.

On the positive side, we're still not too old to be excited by the challenge of making it all work again.

As for the second principle of never taking your employees for granted, it's something we feel strongly about. Our employees are the unsung heroes and heroines of our operation and we let them know that by relating to them with respect, dignity, openess, and honesty. A few years ago I was part of a group of industry people who developed the theme "America's Hospitality Industry: Ours is a Special World." We even put that logo (the printers call it a bug) on our stationery. We try to make our people feel that our operation is special because *they* are working here. In turn, we try to convey that our industry is special, which reflects on our employees. Not everyone can do what they do. We have found that never taking anyone or anything for granted is a pretty good business creed to live by.

Steer Clear Of The Minefields

Jerry L. Hill is Chief Executive Officer of Bill Knapps of Michigan, Inc., a chain of family dinnerhouse restaurants headquartered in Battle Creek, Michigan. He is a past Chairman of the Board of the Michigan Restaurant Association.

Question: For a person entering the hospitality industry, what pitfalls would you caution them to avoid?

If you're interested in developing leadership skills and tackling leadership responsibility, you'd be hard pressed to find another field that offers more opportunity than the restaurant industry. Not only are many leadership positions available, but those positions are likely to be true leadership roles.

Employees are often newcomers to the job force and need tremendous mentoring. Others are part-time workers with other jobs competing for their energy and skills. Further, these employees must, at times, function without the leader being on the premises. Leadership in the foodservice industry is challenging.

Listening to veterans of the foodservice industry describe their experience sounds strikingly familiar to veterans describing war. And, if operating a restaurant is tantamount to being at war, the leader's role is similar to being a minesweeper. Much like the minesweeper, the restaurant leader must be out in front of the troops leading the team through treacherous ground. Some of the mines to be avoided are labeled poor food. Others are labeled poor service. Perhaps the most treacherous are tagged poor leadership. Let's take a look at the leadership mines you can encounter along the way.

An Energy Level That's Anything but HIGH

Certainly the first mine you would discover is called Energy Level. The foodservice industry has often been described as fast paced. We think it's even faster than that. In our segment, midscale dining, the guests expect their meals to be served promptly. In the quick-service segment, guests expect their meals to be served instantly. You have to move quickly to get the job done and to display a critical sense of urgency for your employees.

If working quickly isn't challenging itself, working quickly all the time will be. Many restaurants are open 24 hours. Those that aren't seem like they are to their managers. A typical restaurant manager works approximately ten hours per day. Though difficult at first, you'll eventually become accustomed to working 25 percent more hours than your typical eight hour-per-day friends.

Frequently, you must be on premises for two or more meal periods. Often you will work Friday, Saturday, and Sunday, most holidays, and every Mother's Day, the busiest day in the industry. If you want to join the Foodservice Industry, you'd better check with Mom.

To many, what's most disturbing about the hours in the Foodservice Industry is how varied they can be. You'll be required to start work at a different time several days a week. You'll be called in on your day off to cover for employees who don't show. You'll stay late to address problems that must be resolved immediately. There is little certainty in the industry about the hours except that they're usually long and always unpredictable.

To meet the challenge of long, weekend and varied hours you must have a tremendous level of energy.

Service is an Intangible Product

At the end of these long days, it's important to reflect on your work and take satisfaction in doing your job well. In the restaurant industry, it's often difficult to see the fruits of your labor. You may be in an empty restaurant, perhaps only in the company of the night clean up person, with no concrete evidence of your daily accomplishment except for sore feet and a tie with ketchup on it. Those in other industries, offices and production facilities, for example, can often point to their output: reams of typed papers, cars built, etc. In the foodservice industry it isn't that way.

Service is an intangible product and exists only in the mind of our employees (hopefully) and, more importantly, our guests. For leaders in the foodservice industry, it's a smile on a guest's face at the end of a meal and it's offering good food at a competitive price.

Leaders in the foodservice industry must look to their service to take pride in their work. Though it's much more difficult to take pride in a service than in a product, it's no less satisfying.

You Must Truly Enjoy People

"I'm a people person" is probably the most often told lie in the foodservice industry (heard only slightly more frequently than "Your order is coming right up"). Most people entering the industry are in for a surprise when they find out just how much "a people person" they need to be.

For your guests, you must listen even when you don't want to. This happens often. After working four hours on your day off when you planned to be at the beach, it will be difficult to listen to guests describe problems with their food and service. You'll think the guests should be grateful you made a personal sacrifice for them; however, they'll merely be interested in the superior food and service they deserve.

Complaints are not the only guest comments that are difficult to listen to. Even the compliments can compete with your other priorities. When paperwork is piling up, it's hard to visit with a guest to hear how your restaurant serves the finest tenderloin steak in town. You will often have priorities that will compete with guest contact. With few exceptions, you must devote your attention to the guest when the priorities conflict.

Leadership requires constant contact with customers, monitoring their needs, and listening to feedback on your performance and that of your staff. As you advance in the foodservice industry, contact with the customer decreases only slightly. Though you may have increasing administrative responsibilities, these will be in addition to the contact you have with the customers. Though you may have responsibilities in the office, you will never operate primarily out of an office. It's essential to be on the restaurant floor directing your employee team and visiting with the guests.

No Complaints Doesn't Mean No Complaints

Some foodservice leaders strive to have a day when no guest complains about any element of his or her visit. No condition could be more misleading. If you don't have any guest complaints, you probably don't have any guests.

Live mines are always lurking out there waiting for you to get overconfident, drop your guard, and step directly on them. If you're not getting complaints about your food or service, your monitoring system for entertaining guest concerns is not functioning properly.

It's virtually impossible to please everyone all the time so you must sample guest satisfaction continually. Most people who are dissatisfied with a visit to your establishment will never tell you. You must solicit opinion by observing the operation, maintaining close contact with your employees, and asking guests point blank.

Never is Everything in Order

Leading a team of foodservice employees is a task that requires massive, constant effort. It's a never ending task somewhat similar to painting the Golden Gate bridge. Painting that famous landmark is continuous. As soon as the paint at one end of the bridge is dry, the ironwork at the other end needs repainting.

In the same way, devoting time and effort to the many areas of a restaurant operation is a never-ending task. You can be assured that any of the following beliefs are as phony as mock-turtle soup; you have enough line staff, your staff is sufficiently trained, your service can't be improved, your food can't be improved. Attention to these tasks must be continuous. Be suspicious of comfortable feelings. You're probably not receiving accurate feedback.

Focus On Your Current Position

In the foodservice industry, there is tremendous opportunity for advancement. Sometimes, this opportunity breeds impatience in industry newcomers. Don't look at the next leadership position or responsibility until you can excel in your present job. And the operative word is "excel." You must perform in a superior way to move up, not merely at an acceptable level.

Flexibility

Flexibility is central to effectively leading a restaurant. Most anyone can hit a fastball, but you'll receive a steady diet of curves, knucklers, change-ups and screwballs. Equipment breaks down, competitors steal employees you've spent months training, and just when you revamp your menu, guests' tastes will change. Roll with the punches and you'll avoid getting hit.

Some problems can be anticipated and, therefore, can be managed. Others are unavoidably sudden and devastating. You must allow time for unscheduled emergencies because they're going to happen. When you create a work schedule that prevents you from attending to important matters with little notice, you're likely to suffer the effects.

Vince Lombardi

It's a shame that Vince Lombardi has never opened a restaurant like so many recent sports figures have, because Vince would be a good restaurateur. As a coach of the Green Bay Packers, Lombardi's philosophy was: The team that best accomplished the basics of blocking and tackling, will be the winner.

Our company founder, Bill Knapp, was a fan of Vince Lombardi and believed in much the same philosophy. The restaurant that best accomplishes the basics, top quality food, hospitable service, will be successful. Anytime food and service aren't the top two priorities, you're on a collision course with a mine.

Commitment

Without commitment, you will fail. Until you are committed, you will be hesitant. You will draw back and not realize your potential effectiveness. The moment you become committed to the hospitality industry in general and to your specific assignment you are well on the road to success and reward. The hospitality industry demands great sacrifices which are offset by great rewards. Steer clear of the minefields, apply the Golden Rule to all employees and guests, and be committed to your job. This industry is a great choice.

The leadership path is fraught with pitfalls. Anticipating these pitfalls is a tremendous step toward avoiding them. The successful restaurant leader will surely make contact with these obstacles at some point, for exposure to them is part of the learning process. Recognizing that these pitfalls are numerous and inevitable and managing your reaction to them will make you a successful leader.

Be A Personable People Person

Rodney G. Stoner is the Director of Food and Beverage for the Greenbrier, a world renowned vacation and health resort located in White Sulpher Springs, West Virginia.

Question: For a person entering the hospitality industry, what pitfalls would you caution them to avoid?

Since I have a college age son and daughter who both aspire to a career in the hospitality industry, I have focused on this question in a very personal way.

When embarking on any new endeavor, it has been my experience that an individual's personality and background have an ultimate impact on his or her success or failure. When I interview a young person who is entering our industry, I try to assess the individual's quality standards, knowledge of our industry, and background. In turn, when advising them of the opportunities available, I encourage those individuals to seek out those businesses with good management teams, high quality standards, and good growth potential. Possible pitfalls will be minimized if the employer offers a quality package.

I have several recommendations for avoiding pitfalls in the initial stages of employment. It is vital that new employees know their peers and understand the importance of a team effort. Our industry is a people-oriented business, so sharpening people skills is a priority. Too often pitfalls occur when the employee focuses too much attention on his or her own role and neglects the importance of interaction with fellow workers.

Paramount in the learning process is the ability to seek out quality time both on and off the job. I encourage individuals to think through daily tasks and take time to assess productivity at the end of each day.

Patience is a virtue, and pitfalls often occur when an individual acts in haste, is over-zealous to succeed, and does not realize the importance of teamwork.

Happiness is one of the most important factors in life, both personally and professionally. The hospitality industry is a demanding career, one that often conflicts with family, friends, and personal interests. In order to balance one's professional and personal commitments, it is essential to prioritize your work time. The hospitality industry is a twenty-four hour a day business and it is vital that an individual learn to manage his or her lifestyle early in one's career.

My final recommendation relates to the true definition of hospitality and what it represents in our industry. The basics of hospitality include being nice, making yourself available, having a genuine interest in people, and offering customers quality experiences. Whether that experience is staying in a hotel for one night or ten nights, dining on steak or hamburger, or drinking cola or champagne, it is essential that the experience is a positive one. Focus on the customer. Assess how the decisions you make and the planning you do affect the customer and your fellow workers. Take time to review your decisions in relationship to the customer's satisfaction. When you are able to focus on those factors that make your guests return to your place of business, then you will avoid the pitfalls that result from complacency and mediocrity.